HEAVEN'S
The Diary of an Extra

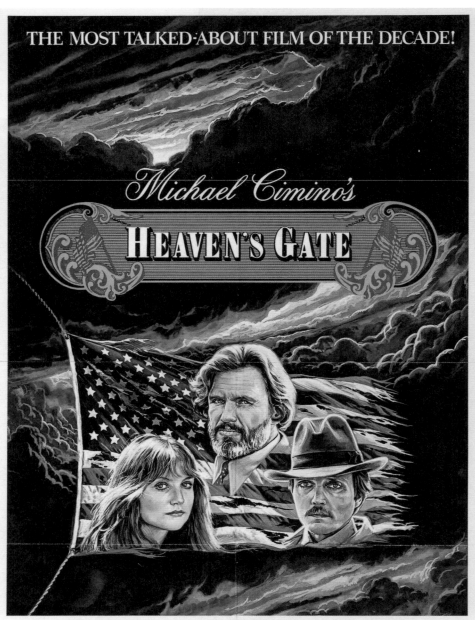

THE MOST TALKED-ABOUT FILM OF THE DECADE!

Michael Cimino's

HEAVEN'S GATE

KRIS KRISTOFFERSON IN MICHAEL CIMINO'S HEAVEN'S GATE

CO-STARRING CHRISTOPHER WALKEN · JOHN HURT · SAM WATERSTON · BRAD DOURIF

ISABELLE HUPPERT AS ELLA · JOSEPH COTTEN AS THE REVEREND DOCTOR · ALSO STARRING JEFF BRIDGES

MUSIC BY DAVID MANSFIELD · DIRECTOR OF PHOTOGRAPHY VILMOS ZSIGMOND, A.S.C. · PRODUCED BY JOANN CARELLI · WRITTEN AND DIRECTED BY MICHAEL CIMINO

70mm Six-Track

HEAVEN'S GATE
The Diary of an Extra

VIVIAN RIDLER

Edited by Colin Ridler
Foreword by Nicolas Kent of Oxford Films

THE PERPETUA PRESS
OXFORD

Half-title page: Vivian Ridler, wearing his *Heaven's Gate* attire,
stands in Catte Street during filming of the movie's prologue
in Oxford, April 1980. Sand and peat have been deposited
to obscure the street's modern tarmac.
Frontispiece: Isabelle Huppert, Kris Kristofferson and
Christopher Walken – the love triangle in the story – are
given prominence in one of the later posters for the movie.

EDITOR'S NOTE

Shortly after retiring from Oxford University Press
– where he had been Printer to the University 1958-78 –
my father, Vivian Ridler, signed on as an extra for the opening
scenes of the Hollywood movie *Heaven's Gate* that were being shot in
Oxford. The amusing and well-informed diary he kept is printed here
in Part I, much as he wrote it. Part II has been added by the Editor
to fill out the background to the entire movie and how its director,
Michael Cimino, came to make such a vastly expensive blockbuster.
Its catastrophic reception in 1980 helped bring about the end of an
era of directorial autonomy, giving the story a wider significance.
Cimino's career never recovered: Part II ends with discussion of all
his later films. Part III then briefly describes Vivian's own accomplished 8mm films. My old friend Edward Wates, who has charge
of the Perpetua Press imprint, has kindly permitted its use for this
publication. Wise advice, encouragement and help have been given
in particular by Roger Alton, Paul Freestone, Nic Jones, Thomas
Neurath, Daniel Whistler and my sisters Jane Scott and Kate Wilson.
Ben Ridler has again proved a true 'brother-in-arms' during the
book's creation and after. Sincere thanks to Richard Deal at Dexter
Premedia who helped immeasurably with the realization of the book.
Neil Palfreyman's expert assistance with origination of the illustrations
is much appreciated; so too is Hilary Bird's professional index.
Both picture researcher Sally Nicholls and designer
Karin Fremer have been a joy to work with.

A CIP catalogue record for this book is available from the British Library

ISBN 978-1-870882-25-5

Further copies of this book may be obtained by contacting Ben Ridler:
b.ridler@talktalk.net or Colin Ridler: colin.ridler@gmail.com

Designed and typeset in Century Schoolbook
and Superclarendon by Karin Fremer
Printed in Great Britain by Gomer Press Ltd,
Llandysul, Ceredigion, Wales

CONTENTS

Foreword by Nicolas Kent ... 6

PART I

THE DIARY ... 9

PART II

THE MOVIE AND ITS DIRECTOR ... 45

Introduction ... 47

Film Credits for *Heaven's Gate* ... 56

The Plot ... 57

The Making and Unmaking of
Heaven's Gate: A Chronology ... 67

Cimino, Zsigmond and the Stars on *Heaven's Gate* ... 80

The Critics on *Heaven's Gate* ... 88

The Films of Michael Cimino ... 102

PART III

VIVIAN RIDLER: MOVIE BUFF AND
ACCOMPLISHED AMATEUR FILMMAKER ... 111

Genesis of a Passion and Key Films ... 112

The Films of Vivian Ridler: A Chronological List ... 119
Further Reading ... 123
Sources of Illustrations ... 124
Index ... 125

FOREWORD

When, like Vivian, I applied to be an extra in a Hollywood movie shooting in Oxford, it was a casual, spontaneous act of curiosity. I had no idea it would change my life.

Because the scenes filmed in Oxford, doubling for Harvard University, were at the tail end of a monstrously extended schedule, rumours were already circulating that *Heaven's Gate* was very badly over budget. Consequently, in addition to the army of technicians and extras, there was a corps of nervous accountants from the studio, United Artists, whose stern expressions did nothing to mask that their chances of reining in the director, Michael Cimino, were precisely zero. Sanctified by multiple Oscars for *The Deer Hunter*, Cimino had spent far in excess of his allotted budget on *Heaven's Gate* in the belief, sadly mistaken, that his masterpiece was too big and beautiful to fail.

Watching him from the sidelines, I observed that Cimino was a short, Napoleonic figure who spoke quietly in conclave with his actors and cinematographer, but otherwise ignored the chaos which swirled around him including the killer glare of the studio accountants. His nickname among the crew was the Ayatollah Cimino.

But by the time we extras joined this epic, faith in the merits of the movie as a masterpiece in the making was very much alive. That's what its star, Kris Kristofferson, told me when, by chance, Cimino positioned me in front of him in the audience for John Hurt's incomprehensible speech, which Vivian describes so vividly, in the Sheldonian Theatre. My moment of screen glory was almost immediately snatched away when the cinematographer, Vilmos Zsigmond, lined up his shot and unkindly complained I was too short.

Up until then, Kristofferson and I had been happily chatting during these interminable preparations (turns out he'd been a Rhodes scholar and a boxing Blue – in fact, his old boxing coach was also an extra). Summary dismissal was miraculously averted when my new best friend said the magic words: 'Put wedges in the kid's shoes.' Thus providing me with both a reprieve and, in another life, the title of my autobiography.

Kristofferson, a big star – whose career, like United Artists itself, was a casualty of *Heaven's Gate*'s eventual critical mauling and audience indifference – had no doubt that Cimino was making a masterpiece. It's easy to dismiss his faith, but he was no fool. Just another example of how impossible it is to anticipate success in the creative crapshoot of moviemaking in which, famously, 'nobody knows anything'.

Unlike Kristofferson, Cimino and countless studio executives, my own career, which as an undergraduate didn't exist, was blessed rather than cursed by *Heaven's Gate*. After the production wrapped and the circus moved on, I started a student film magazine which I continued to publish after graduating, then switched to making documentaries. Ten years after the filming of the movie which broke United Artists, I was in Los Angeles making a BBC documentary series about the movie business, called *Naked Hollywood*. I happened to be invited to a small drinks party at Universal Studios and among the guests I spied Michael Cimino. I tentatively introduced myself as an extra on *Heaven's Gate*. He beamed. 'It's always a pleasure', he said, 'to meet an alumnus of *Heaven's Gate*.' Thirty years later I'm still struck by his choice of the word, alumnus.

NICOLAS KENT is founder and Creative Director of Oxford Films, an independent production company which has made more than 300 hours of documentaries, drama and films, winning numerous awards including 6 BAFTAs. His first documentary series, *Naked Hollywood*, was described by *Newsweek* as 'the zippiest, funniest, warts-and-all-est look at the American movie business ever seen on TV' and by *Variety* as 'a connoisseur's delight'.

9 April, Wednesday. Up at 5.15 to be at Aldens by 6.
Chilly air, half-moon still shining. Marquees all lit up
when I arrived. Two papers thrust into my hand, one a
seating plan of the Sheldonian showing my place, the
other the usual form indemnifying the company for
all claims against them. Food and drink was ready
in one marquee, but we were told to go through it to
the wardrobe tent and change first. It contained a
heater blower which was turned off almost as I arrived
and didn't come on again. I soon togged myself up
and chatted with those acquaintances who had been
at Pinewood, including the professor, who had stayed
overnight at a friend's in the Iffley Road. We then
had breakfast — eggs, bacon, and coffee before the
long, long process of hanging around while other
'artistes' arrived from London, B'ham & elsewhere.
   In spite of my astrakhan waistcoat I suffered
from the cold — in fact I did so all day. After almost
3 hours waiting around we were at last ushered
into coaches by the innumerable 'assistant directors'
or dogsbodies, and reached the Sheldonian at about
ten past nine. We filed inside, to find the whole
place ablaze with lights, all of them high up and
directed towards the chancellor's seat at the east
end. Three Panavision cameras were already in
position; a fourth was on a crane outside the south [west]
doors, ready to move along a track towards them.

A page from Vivian's handwritten *Diary of an Extra*.

PART I

THE DIARY

Long queue for extras

Five hundred Oxford people are being hired as extras for the film.

Hundreds of hopefuls turned up at auditions in Oxford on Saturday, and director Michael Cimino is now sifting their photographs in preparation for the start of filming on April 8.

"We will be filming in Oxford for aboout two weeks over Easter, and we will be using about 800 extras," said second assistant director Andy Armstrong during Saturday's auditions.

"About 300 extras will be professionals from London but the rest will be students and about 160 older people from Oxford: local people tend to look much better on film because they don't look like professionals. The response to the auditions has been very good."

Extras in the film will receive £15 a day, together with free meals at a massive base camp to be set up in Aldens Field, off Abingdon road, for the two weeks' filming.

A news item in the *Oxford Times* reports the auditioning for *Heaven's Gate* extras.

EARLY IN MARCH 1980, an advertisement appeared in the *Oxford Times* calling for several hundred extras to take part during April in a film called *Heaven's Gate*. No other details were given. Auditions were to be held on a Saturday afternoon and evening in the debating hall of the Oxford Union.

Thinking that it would be fun, as well as interesting, to take part, I duly went along. I got there at about 6, to find the hall empty except for three representatives, all young men, from the film company. I was asked to complete a form ('Are you a member of Equity?' was the only unusual question), two polaroid photographs were then taken, and that was it. I then asked a few questions. Who was the Director? Michael Cimino (of *The Deer Hunter* fame). What was the film about? A war between two late 19th-century cattle barons. What were my chances of being taken on? Very good. And that was that.

From another issue of the *Oxford Times* I learnt that the main part would be taken by Kris Kristofferson; and that Mansfield College had been chosen as a location to do duty for Harvard University at that time. A wall was being built on the Mansfield Road frontage to screen off the road and the modern buildings opposite. A large beech tree (shown in a photo accompanying the article) had been 'planted' in the quadrangle with the aid of a large, very large, crane. To get it there, most of the main branches had been cut off, and were to be bolted back on after the main trunk had been secured. Leaves would then follow...

The following week I was told by telephone that I had not been selected. I was rather disappointed, particularly when I learned that a Teddy Hall colleague, Norman Pollock, had been – and would be paid £15 for every day he worked. Anne[1] assured me that people always dropped out, and I still had a good chance; but I was sceptical. I did, though, go along to Mansfield College to see what they were doing. The tree, more or less branchless, was in position, held in place by steel cables. The branches lay around on the grass. The wall, made of fibreglass on plywood constructions to give the shape of buttresses and pediments, was practically complete, and looked quite convincing in a tatty sort of way. Architecturally it was really rather odd: two grandiose gateways, each complete with heavy-looking timber doors, stood side-by-side within 15 feet of each other; and each capped by the arms of Harvard University. Perhaps the illogical arrangement will be lost by skilful camera work.

23 March, Sunday

A call from the film people to say that I was after all needed, and could I go to Pinewood on Wednesday for a costume fitting. A coach would leave from Alden's in the Abingdon Road at 7 a.m. and we might be at the studios for most of the day. Luckily I was free and said yes. I had also to be available for filming from 8 to 25 April.

26 March, Wednesday

Up at 6, to get to Alden's without too much of a scramble. It was misty and cold at that hour, but I decided to cycle because I was not sure whether I would be able to leave the car in Alden's car park while we were away.

When I arrived, most of the party were there, standing by the coach. I must say that at first sight I thought we looked more ex-Labour Exchange than ex-the groves of academe; but I had

---

1 Anne Ridler, Vivian's wife.

CALL SHEET   NO: 17

PRODUCTION:	"HEAVEN'S GATE"	**DATE:**	Wednesday 9 April 1980
DIRECTOR:	MICHAEL CIMINO	**UNIT CALL:**	8.00am on location
		CAMERA:	8.00am
SET:	INT CHAPEL - SHELDONIAN	**SOUND:**	8.00am
	(SHOOTING)	**PROPS:**	8.00am
		ELECTRICAL:	8.00am
SC. NOS:	2. Day.	**S/BYS:**	8.00am

PRODUCTION NOTE: THERE WILL BE NO SMOKING, NO FOOD, NO DRINKS, AT ANY TIME IN THE SHELDONIAN. PLEASE TREAT THE SHELDONIAN WITH THE UTMOST CARE AND RESPECT.

LOCATION: Sheldonian Theatre Broad Street, Oxford

CONTACT: Mr Raymond Francis
TEL: Oxford 41023

ARTISTE	CHARACTER	D/R	P/UP	M/UP HAIR WARDROBE	ON SET
KRIS KRISTOFFERSON	AVERILL	CARAVAN	7.15am	7.30am	9.00am
JOHN HURT	IRVINE	CARAVAN	7.15am	7.30am	9.00am
JOSEPH COTTEN	REVEREND DOCTOR	CARAVAN	7.00am	8.00am	9.00am
ROSEANNE VELA	ROSIE	CARAVAN	6.00am	6.30am	9.00am
JUDI TROTT	DANCER	CARAVAN	6.00am	6.30am	9.00am
ROBERT FABER	BATON MAN	CARAVAN	7.15am	7.30am	9.00am
TERRY GILBERT	DANCER	CARAVAN	6.30am	7.00am	9.00am
PAUL HILLYER	DANCER	CARAVAN	6.30am	7.00am	9.00am
MARTIN CUTLER	DANCER	CARAVAN	6.30am	7.00am	9.00am
KATE CASTLE	DANCER	CARAVAN	5.30am	6.00am	9.00am
MARION BETZOLD	DANCER	CARAVAN	5.30am	6.00am	9.00am
JULIA SIMONNE	DANCER	CARAVAN	5.30am	6.00am	9.00am
CAROL BEDFORD	DANCER	CARAVAN	5.30am	6.00am	9.0am
WENDY DAWSON	DANCER	CARAVAN	5.30am	6.00am	9.00am

STANDINS:

JACK DEARLOVE for	MR KRISTOFFERSON		8.00am
JACK ROSS for	MR HURT		8.00am
NED LYNCH for	MR COTTEN		8.00am
SUZANNE HEIMER for	MISS VELA		8.00am
SUE BEST for	MISS TROTT		8.00am

EXTRA ARTISTES:

		WHERE FROM			
49 LADIES	RELATIVES	OXFORD	-	6.00am	9.00am
25 MEN	RELATIVES	OXFORD	-	6.00am	9.00am
12 MEN	POLICEMEN	F.A.A.	5.00am	6.15am	9.00am
13 MEN	BANDMEN	ARMY	6.00am	7.15am	9.00am
93 LADIES	DANCERS	F.A.A.	5.00am	6.15am	9.00am
93 MEN	DANCERS	F.A.A.	5.00am	6.15am	9.00am
46 LADIES	RELATIVES/ACADEMICS	F.A.A.	5.00am	6.15am	9.00am
70 MEN	RELATIVES/ACADEMICS	F.A.A.	5.00am	6.15am	9.00am
50 MEN	SENIOR STUDENTS	OXFORD	-	6.30am	9.00am
67 MEN	JUNIORS	F.A.A./ OXFORD	5.00am	6.30am	9.00am
67 MEN	SOPHOMORES	OXFORD	-	6.30am	9.00am
67 MEN	FRESHMEN	OXFORD	-	6.30am	9.00am
47 LADIES	DANCERS	EQUITY	6.00am	7.15am	9.00am
47 MEN	DANCERS	EQUITY	6.00am	7.15am	9.00am
1 MAN	PHOTOGRAPHER	-	-	7.15am	9.00am

TOTAL: 742 PEOPLE

PROD/ASST DIRECTORS: Senior Students, Juniors, Band required for rehearsal at the Sheldonian once completed wardrobe etc.

/ Continued 2

One of numerous call sheets for the Oxford shoot that Vivian collected.

Norman Pollock as a companion on the journey, which passed pleasantly enough.

I was a bit vague as to where Pinewood was. It is in fact not all that far from Denham, and most of the journey is made on the M40. The studios themselves occupy part of what was once Iver Heath, and when you get past the main gates, with their whiff of garden suburb, you soon find yourself creeping through a pretty dreary bunch of industrial buildings which seem to have grown haphazardly, rather like the Radcliffe Infirmary.

But that impression is partly dispelled when you have had time to look around. There is one enormous, new-looking stage called 007, where the Bond films have been made; and the administration block is tolerable in a banal sort of way.

We were ushered into a vast, run-down looking stage, which had been divided down the middle for LADIES and MEN (sic). In our section were racks and racks of clothing, top-hats, beavers, and other sombre wear befitting a 19th-century university. Of course we had to wait about while each of us was fitted and photographed; but the waiting was not tedious to those of us who had brought books or found interesting companions to talk to. I was amused as well as surprised to find among the party one of my old comps,[2] Fred White, who had retired early because of ill-health. In his long coat and topper he looked positively cadaverous, poor chap, but he may be just what they are looking for.

Apart from Pollock, I found myself talking to a congenial man called John Crabtree. He is a professor of chemistry who has spent a good part of his working life in Thailand and Ethiopia. He returned to Britain two years ago and has been unable to find a job since. He lives at Haddenham, where he earns a little money working at home translating Pergamon Press manuscripts into Russian, a language he learnt when he was in the services. He is worried about getting into Oxford by 7 a.m., if that is to be the regular calling time because, as he put it, his car is 'out of use'.

---

2 Compositors, at the University Press, Oxford, where Vivian had been Printer until his retirement in 1978.

I asked him whether he knew the Norringtons.[3] He said he did, and then added 'you're not *the* Vivian Ridler, are you?', to which I made the suitably humble, appropriate, and modest reply, at the same time hoping for stardom.

When my turn came, I found myself in the hands of an amiable, large, Jewish-looking tailor. He soon produced a white shirt, black cravat, to be worn knotted, a splendid astrakhan waistcoat, a well-fitting long coat, and a rather tight-fitting topper. I put them on, but before I went to be photographed I asked him whether all this gear belonged to Pinewood or came from Moss Bros. He told me that Moss Bros could not have coped with all the costumes needed (some 750 I gathered), and that they had been hired from several suppliers in different parts of the country. He added that 'this little lot will probably cost the company about £40,000 to hire'. As they have apparently spent some $40 million[4] on the picture already, I suppose this is nothing very much. We are, he said, needed for the prologue and epilogue to the film, and Cimino himself was on the stage next door rehearsing some dance that takes place during the Harvard sequences. When I said that I wouldn't be surprised if all our scenes ended on the cutting-room floor, he said it was highly unlikely because the rest of the film had already been shot.

He asked me whether I lived in Oxford. He then told me that he had last been in the Oxford area for Billy Wilder's *Private Life of Sherlock Holmes* (1969), with Robert Stephens as S.H. They had shot a long boat-race sequence, again with a large crowd of extras, specially made oars and other refinements, and in the end none of it had been used in the final cut.

Then, specs off, I was photographed and numbered. Tents have been put up in Alden's Field, and all the costumes and fittings will be held there. We shall change and be taken to the locations and back again by coach.

---

3 Sir Thomas (ALP) Norrington (1899-1982), a family friend, was Secretary to the Delegates at Oxford University Press 1948-54, and President of Trinity College, Oxford 1954-70.
4 The original budget had been $11.5 million, but in the end it spiralled to $36 million, or $44 million including promotion costs. See Part II.

A large sign announced that all men must have short hair or be prepared to have it cut. We were advised to go to the temporary hairdressing saloon set up alongside for a check and possibly a free haircut. The saloon was run by two fairly fearsome young- ish women, who severed many a lush lock from the heads of our party. I had rather a lengthy wait because (a) they were just off for a coffee break, and (b) when they returned they decided to deal with several of the young ladies who had been sent along from the LADIES section. Some were in crinolines, all were very young, and most of them were very pretty. They certainly looked charming when they came along to be photographed by our camera-man. I think most of them had been hired from ballet schools, as several were involved in the dance rehearsals.

The hairdresser thought my hair short enough, but I persuaded her that with her skill she should be able to work wonders, which she did.

At the end of the morning we were told that the paymaster and the cafeteria were in the Admin. Block. We sidled down a long corridor, past a fine large-scale model of a ship with 'Texas Rose, Boston' painted on her stern, to the office where we were each handed £15 against our Artistes Salary Vouchers.

The cafeteria was at the other end. A large room, nearly full when we got there, but we didn't have to wait long, and ended up with excellent ham omelettes and veg. at very low prices.

Over lunch John Crabtree told me that he had left Addis Ababa when he became increasingly insecure. After Haile Selassie had been deposed and the military installed he had suddenly been taken off to prison. He was not held long, but he felt particularly the humiliation of having his spectacles removed (without them he is virtually blind), and his shoelaces. He was kept in a small cell with about 20 others, all Ethiopians. The day after he was released several of them had been taken out and shot. They had even shot a seven-year old schoolboy for 'Deviationism'. Most hor- rible of all, he had witnessed the massacre of about 1800 students from the university. A ban had been put on all demonstrations, but they insisted on a protest march against the so-called Marxist regime for not being Marxist enough. The soldiers had ordered them to break up, and when they did not, simply mowed them down with machine guns. Crabtree said he still felt the effects of what he had seen, and no wonder. He is now going to try for a job in Zimbabwe.

Finally, when we returned to our coach we were told that we would be called for Wednesday, 9 April, when our location would be the Sheldonian. We were back in Oxford by 3.45, accompanied on the way by the voice of the Chancellor, Geoffrey Howe, making his grim budget speech to a noisy House of Commons.

30 March, Sunday

After the Palm Sunday morning service at St Mary's, I went along to Mansfield College to see whether anything was afoot. I found the tree specialists at work putting on the branches that had been severed for transit. The work was being done with the aid of the giant crane and with cables held by men on the ground. At the far side of the quad a new wall had been put up, awaiting the scenic experts to weather it in the convincing way that the street wall had been dealt with. A lone policeman appeared to be on duty in the quad, or perhaps, like me, he had been drawn there by curiosity.

5 April, Saturday

Anne took a call from the film people to say that I was to be at Alden's Field by 6 a.m. on Wednesday. They must be taking no chances over starting work on time, whatever time that may be.

6 April, Sunday

After the Easter Day service at St Mary's we drove Janet Butler (whom we had brought down from her home because Ted Butler is unwell) to show her what had been done at Mansfield College. The tree now has both branches and leaves, and the grass has been replaced around the base of the trunk. The wall and arch on the far side are in position, tho' not yet completely finished. Another short stretch of wall has been added at the front, sealing off the quad from the road. Other work has also been started, but it is too early to discern what is intended.

The vicar's wife told me that they had seen two mobile lavatories being put into position beyond the quad. They arrived labelled 'Ladies' and 'Gentlemen', but later this had been altered to 'Women' and 'Men'!

9 April, Wednesday

Up at 5.15 to be at Alden's by 6. Chilly air, half-moon still shining, marquees all lit up when I arrived. Two papers thrust into my hand, one a seating plan of the Sheldonian showing my place, the other the usual form indemnifying the company for all claims against them. Food and drink was ready in one marquee, but we were told to go through it to the wardrobe tent and change first. It contained a heater blower which was turned off almost as I arrived and didn't come on again. I soon togged myself up and chatted with those acquaintances who had been at Pinewood, including the professor, who had stayed overnight at a friend's in the Iffley Road. We then had breakfast – eggs, bacon, coffee – before the long, long process of hanging around while other 'artistes' arrived from London, Birmingham and elsewhere.

In spite of my astrakhan waistcoat I suffered from the cold – in fact I did so all day. After almost 3 hours waiting around we were at last ushered into coaches by the innumerable 'assistant directors' or dogsbodies, and reached the Sheldonian at about 10 past 9. We filed inside, to find the whole place ablaze with lights, all of them high up and directed towards the chancellor's seat at the north end. Three Panavision cameras were already in position; a fourth was on a crane outside the south doors, ready to move along a track towards them. The adults, men and women, were almost all seated at the north ground-floor level and the lower gallery. A few adults were sprinkled among the 'young bloods' in the upper gallery. Members of the Class of '70, taking part in what was to be some kind of university chapel ceremony, stood in ranks on the main floor, divided by the main gangway leading from the southern entrance. These wretched young men had to stand there throughout the morning and afternoon, which most of the professional extras mixed in with us thought a piece of ineptness on the part of the assistant directors, who spent a lot of energy in telling us to keep quiet, *please.*

While we were sitting and waiting we watched the horde of specialists, camera crews, make-up men, women hairdressers, stand-ins, property men, swarming around like bees. I asked the continuity girl to point out the director of photography, Vilmos Zsigmond (highly praised for his work on *The Deer Hunter*), to me. She said she would when he next came along. Meanwhile I turned to my neighbour and asked him what he thought a small, lugubrious figure in a blue duffle jacket and a thin bedraggled scarf hanging from his neck did. We both thought he was probably in charge of costumes because he seemed to be scanning the ladies and their bustles and crinolines with particular intensity. Then he was swallowed by other technicians. Almost immediately the continuity girl, who had been taking polaroid stills of the crowd, came back and pointed out Zsigmond. He also is a smallish man, with a lined, humorous, face, and a beard – really the most, per- haps the only, distinguished-looking man among the technicians. I then said, 'And I suppose that is Cimino?', pointing to a tallish man, also with a beard, and wearing a blue-white sports cap. 'No', she said, 'there's Cimino, behind Zsigmond, that man in the blue duffle coat and a scarf.' Shock! He certainly looked the most insig- nificant man in the place. Throughout the day he left the talking and instruction to the assistants, just watching the proceedings, occasionally talking with Joseph Cotten, Kristofferson, and John Hurt, or looking through one of the cameras to check a set-up.

The Panavision camera (*above*) is lined up for external shots, while (*opposite*) Cimino directs John Hurt, with Kris Kristofferson, his back towards us, in the foreground and assistant director Brian Cook striding to the left.

I was told later by one of the actors that he knew exactly what he wanted, had already instructed and rehearsed the actors and assistants elsewhere, and could therefore concentrate on watching to see that they did what had been agreed.

The director of photography was moving around, very calmly, most of the time, checking light readings and having minor adjustments made to the lights. He seemed to say very little to the camera crews, who I suppose had already been told what lenses and angles to choose. What seemed a bit of typical film-world extravagance was the large translucent plastic awning which the prop men spent most of the morning draping over an elaborate construction of tubular scaffolding outside the south entrance. Later I realized that this had probably been done to balance the sunlight more closely with the interior lighting as the crane camera tracked in.

'there's Cimino, behind Zsigmond, that man in the blue duffle coat and a scarf.' Shock! He certainly looked the most insignificant man in the place.

The first rehearsal shots began about 11.15. We had been amused to see in the galleries when we came in a number of plaster dummy figures placed here and there to swell the crowd. I didn't think they looked convincing against real people, and sure enough Cimino suddenly had them all removed. We saw them in a pile outside, looking rather pathetic.

Much time had been spent by the assistant directors in re-arranging the women and girls in the galleries. Presumably this was done to get a better mix of colours, tho' as one of the d's apologized for the 'balls-up', this may not have been so. Anyway, it took a lot of sorting out, just adding to the tedium, because it was quite impossible to read in such an atmosphere of continual bustle.

None of us were told in any detail what the context of the scene was. The president, the Reverend Doctor (Joseph Cotten), was apparently making a farewell address in Harvard Chapel to the Class of '70. He would then invite their chosen 'class orator', William K Irvine (John Hurt) to make the traditional reply. This would be facetious and impertinent, much to the taste of his class and the bloods in the gallery, but not at all so to the 'academics, relatives' (me), and other elders present, who were to applaud Cotten at certain moments but frown on Hurt and his supporters.

The proceedings were to open with a brass band marching in through the south doors and turning right and left through the west and east gangways as they neared the dais. They would be closely followed by a rabble of student latecomers, Hurt among them, who would noisily take their places as Cotten began his speech. The crane camera would begin low down behind the band, moving in and upwards as the students followed, ending up, as far as I could tell, on Cotten. It should make an effective shot.

We had all been issued with printed 'programmes'. At the end of Hurt's speech these were to be showered down from the top gallery as enthusiastic support.

Both speeches were fairly long, and fairly dull, tho' Hurt's probably had some significance in the plot. They went through them over and over again, with the full proceedings – band entrance

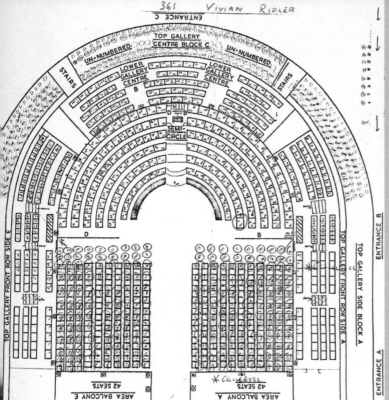

Inside the Sheldonian: John Hurt (*above*) as Class of '70 orator walks across to Joseph Cotten, who as the Reverend Doctor stands with his back towards us; Vivian's annotated plan (*left*) of the seating arrangement marks his own allocated spot with a large red circle.

and student rush – each time. I was interested to note that neither actor gave, or possibly chose to give, the same performance each time; and as the lunch hour passed, the students stood there, and the speeches were made, I thought the actors got worse and worse, with longer and longer pauses and baroque inflections. Cotten's speech opened with 'If this be not a farce', after which there were a few titters from the students. By about the sixth take the titter had developed into a roar, with catcalls. The enthusiasm for Hurt's supposed witticisms also ended in a high pitch of hysteria.

The break for lunch came at 4.15. As I had been moved from my place to make room for a camera I was near the door, and practically led the stampede to Mansfield College and the pre-packed airflight-type meals and hot soup being served in another big marquee at the rear of the college. So I found a seat at one of the tables. Many of those who had been in the top gallery found they had to sit on the floor.

I found room for a pleasant young American who was being paid £50 a day as a dancer, and had been standing among the students since 9 o'clock. He turned out to be a preacher and was doing this for the money. When I told him that the Vicar of St Mary's had turned down the company's request to use the church for the Harvard Chapel after reading the script (a decision much regretted by some members of the PCC[5] who would have welcomed the money for the church coffers), he said that he knew Peter Cornwell (the Vicar) and was himself having doubts about being involved because he had heard that the main part of the film contained a lot of violence and nudity. I couldn't help thinking of Jimmy Durante's line, after he had sung at the piano: 'I know it's lousy, but they pay me for it, so I'm helpless.'[6]

We were called back to the Sheldonian at 5 by the assistants. Their constant refrain was shushing (even 'shut up' at one point) and a warning to remove spectacles and wristwatches. As I can't

5 From a minute of St Mary's Parochial Church Council (which had been asked to permit filming in the church), 11 December 1979: 'The Vicar had recommended against allowing the filming of Heaven's Gate in the church, having read the script in full. He reported the film to be without artistic merit and a crude mixture of sex and violence.'
6 The US singer, comedian and actor Durante's hit song of 1934.

see anything without my glasses I ignored this request and only took them off when I saw a camera pointing or coming my way. It was curious that no one seemed to notice.

While we were at lunch the cameras had been moved in for close-ups, on Cotten and Hurt (those speeches *again!*), and on one of the principals, Roseanne Vela, who had to emote with adoration and amusement, or perhaps just amusement, as Hurt went through his speech. She also had to look longingly towards Kristofferson in the ranks of the students.

The students had revolted during the lunch-break, complaining that they would not work more than nine hours for £15. Thereupon the asst. director hastily announced that a deal had been struck and that for any time after 5 p.m. we would get £2.50 an hour. Cheers all round.

The close-ups were completed by 6.15, not without a ten-minute fiddle with Miss Vela's hairdo and face by a make-up woman, just after the announcement had been made that the cameras were about to roll. Cimino remained alongside the two cameras on Miss V throughout the several takes.

We were then told that all the interior lighting and camera positions were to be arranged for a range of reverse-angle shots. This would take some time, coaches had been sent for so that we could 'relax' in them, and would we all now 'get out'. We did so, most people surging into the King's Arms or the White Hart because it was very cold and no coaches were in sight.

John Hurt told me in the White Hart, where I was crushed to the wall by ladies in crinolines, that Cimino, who was paying £10,000 a day for the Sheldonian, was determined to finish there that night.[7] Which meant we might be around until the small hours. Gloom. But I passed the interval pleasantly enough talking with some of the professional extras, who assured me that filmmaking was not usually as bad as this, it was that the Americans had

---

7 Having lost the battle to rein in Cimino's vast overspend during the previous year's filming in Montana and Wyoming, United Artists, the distributor, threatened to cancel the Oxford shoot unless the proposed budget of $5.2 million for these scenes was reduced to just under $3 million. Uncharacteristically, Cimino acquiesced.

different methods. Actually, I thought the exercise had been quite well organized. Only Cimino could say whether he was satisfied with the takes, and he simply had to get it right.

During this break there was another revolt, this time by Equity. When I came out of the pub, a union meeting was being held outside Blackwell's. Later I heard one of their members saying that they had demanded payment that night: it seemed as though they hadn't been paid for some days and they wanted 'money on the table'. I heard also that many of the dancers were disgruntled because they had been told in January that they would be getting between 10 and 15 days work, and in fact they would be getting only 2 or 3. So the evening mood became distinctly edgy.

The interior was a blaze of light when we returned, most of it directed towards the south side and the main floor. They simulate external daylight in an ingenious way. The upper arcs of the ground-floor windows were covered with translucent plastic. Outside each window were placed banks of about 20 photoflood bulbs on stands, beamed at the window arcs. (All power for the lights is generated in trucks parked along Catte Street.) Inside the effect to the naked eye is quite convincing, and on film will be more so.

The band had to march again, this time starting from inside the closed south doors. They were being picked up by a camera placed at a low level below the chancellor's seat, which seemed also to be aligned on Kristofferson, because it was only during one of these takes that Cimino cut suddenly and had the man in front of K moved forward and touched up by a make-up hand. Otherwise he had let all shots run their course.

We had to endure the speeches several times more so that the principals could be held in frame while the reactions of the students were being recorded. During one of these takes Hurt suddenly began hamming up his speech, ad-libbing and putting on funny voices. He was encouraged in this by the reactions of the young men, but Cotten was obviously embarrassed, and I certainly was. I don't know why he did it. Tiredness and just showing off perhaps.

The band marches in as Cimino (with scarf) and the camera crew supervise the action.

After that take our section was released. The coach was ready (it was then about 9.30), we were quickly back at Alden's, where I changed, was paid off, told to report at 6 the following Tuesday, then went through to the cafeteria for a good supper of sausages, pork chop, quarter of chicken, veg., cheese, fruit and coffee. I felt I'd earned it. The day had been the most curious mixture of fascination and tedium. I was back home soon after 11. Anne had begun to get quite worried because, as she said, she didn't think they could continue filming the daylight scenes after dark. But that's showbiz.

11 April, Friday

A phone message came through yesterday to say that I was wanted this morning at 6.30. A cold damp mist hung over the river as I cycled over Donnington Bridge, and it remained quite cold all day. But this time I had put on an extra jersey so that I fared rather better during the hanging about. We moved to the location, Catte Street and New College Lane, not long after we had changed and had something to eat. We arrived at about 7.15. In the early hours workmen had dumped tons of sand and peat all over the streets. Other young men with rakes and shovels were busy trying to even it out and bring more of the peat to the top. Soon afterwards five carriages, each drawn by a pair of horses, were brought to Catte Street and placed in position, one of them across the road at the Radcliffe Square end to screen the wooden barrier gate from view. The carriages had all been hired from a man near Dunstable who makes a living from TV and film companies.

Convincing-looking name boards had been clipped over the Catte Street and New College Lane signs, one reading Savile Street, the other Huntingdon Road.

The shots turned out to be quite intricate. The brass band, followed by students (including Hurt and Kristofferson) were to march along N. C. Lane towards a camera on a crane, turning right down Catte Street and then left on to the Clarendon Building forecourt. At the same time students who were late, some half-dressed, were to run after the procession from Radcliffe Square and Hertford College while various carriages drove to and fro and the 'academics' and their consorts strolled along in the same direction. Several other cameras were covering the scene, and as there were endless rehearsals and takes, with the band playing 'When the Saints Go Marching In', this one shot took until 1 p.m. to get right. I had been paired with a withered crone as my consort and, as I soon found that she was rather a bore, I spent most of the time between takes in stamping up and down outside Hertford on the pretext of trying to keep warm. Fortunately Anne appeared in Radcliffe Square, which broke the monotony. With her usual saintliness she went back for my ciné-camera, with which I managed a few not all that interesting shots.

The layer of sand and peat was very thick, which made it difficult to walk across. The gutters and pavements were constantly being swept after the carriage wheels had sprayed them. The surface didn't look all that convincing to me – rather like Weston[8] after the tide has gone out – but no doubt it will look passable enough on film.

Anne came down again after lunch, in time to see a rather good backward tracking shot in front of the band as it came through the tunnel arch into the Bodleian courtyard. During one of the takes John Hurt sprained his ankle. A chair was rushed in for him, his shoe and sock stripped off, and his foot and ankle cosseted like an only child. But he couldn't continue, and was carted off to the Radcliffe.

Jane[9] had also come along during the morning and decided to bring the girls down after lunch. I'm afraid it must have been very tedious for them because most of the afternoon was taken up with filming the rear of the band and procession as it marched (out of their sight) along New College Lane. But at least they saw some of the horses and carriages in action.

The last shot of the day was a short tracking one in Queen's Lane. Kristofferson had to sprint up the lane, as tho' catching up with the procession, while a carriage containing one of the principal ladies passed him. While I was standing in the middle of the lane, watching the camera being set up, Cimino called for me to come and stand in front of another carriage which had been placed in front of Lord Blake's door.[10] He asked me to turn my head, watching Kristofferson as he ran past. 'No expression, unless you want to look angry at what we're doing to your road.' He also ordered the props man to fit me with John Hurt's steel glasses, which he

8 Weston-Super-Mare, near Bristol, where Vivian as a boy went to bathe.
9 Jane Länge (now Scott), Vivian and Anne's eldest daughter, with her two young children, Karin and Juliette.
10 Lord (Robert) Blake (1916-2003) was at this time Provost of The Queen's College, Oxford.

Kristofferson had to sprint up the lane . . . while a carriage containing one of the principal ladies passed him. While I was standing in the middle of the lane . . . Cimino called for me to come and stand in front of another carriage . . .

did. Props then said he also had a pair of gold-rimmed ones and went in search of them. When he came back and put them on me he said 'I think they look bloody awful.' I suggested we go over and show Cimino. He took one look and said 'very good'. Collapse of props. I enjoyed this hour because I was close enough to the camera to hear the various comments and exchanges that passed between Cimino and Zsigmond. Altho' Kristofferson's stand-in did the rehearsal sprints, he himself had to do all the others, and it was quite exhausting. The shot was difficult because the camera had to make a short track down the lane as K raced up, stop, and turn as the carriage passed to pick him up in rear shot as he disappeared round the corner into New College Lane. The thick sand made quick running difficult.

That was the end of the day's work. I was paid 4 hours overtime and was home soon after 7.

During the filming on 11 April Vivian (*left*), looking every inch the Harvard Elder, stands in Catte Street, with a coach and horses and the Bodleian Library entrance behind; meantime the band (*below*) marches out of New College Lane on its way into the Sheldonian.

15 April, Tuesday

Another unnecessarily early call, but the air was not so cold as I cycled to Tent City. We were all handed a ground-plan of Mansfield College, including its film-set additions, with the positions of all the extras numbered and marked. My position as a 'relative' was near the main door on the far side of the quad. We were brought to the location soon after 7, and during the long wait before the cameras rolled I had more than enough time to study the preparations that had already been made. A circular track had been put around the tree in the centre, on which 3 cameras, mounted on trolleys, were in position and being adjusted by their crews. The fourth camera, mounted on a tripod, stood on a wooden stage above them. These positions meant that all the takes would be from the inside of the dancing groups which were to dance around the tree to the strains of the 'Blue Danube' on the playback.

A little later the horses and coaches – already used in the Catte Street sequence – arrived. They were placed at the far side of the quad, near to a convincing addition to the college building whose purpose was to screen off the garden beyond.

One of the extras who had worked briefly on Sunday morning told me that he had taken part in a short scene showing Kristofferson running along a stretch of Pembroke Street. The unit was in something of a hurry because they were apparently using the street without authority. Yet they had still covered it with a layer of peat (only, this time). I had gone in search of them on Sunday morning, but in the Queen's Lane area. By one of those odd coincidences I did come upon a film unit around the corner in New College Lane. I didn't recognize any of the faces, and soon discovered that they belonged to a Granada TV unit.

Most of the dancers had assembled in Mansfield by 10, Hurt and Kristofferson soon afterwards. Then shooting began, without rehearsals. We were told to stand back from the gravel path because a carriage and horses, with four elegant women aboard, was to emerge from the farther arch, circle the quad as the dancers danced and we waived and cheered, and disappear through the arch again. After it had passed we were to surge forward to the edge of the lawn giving, and I quote the 2nd assistant director, 'good reactions'.

The playback played the waltz each time, with a deafening noise, the 3 cameras were slowly pushed around the tree at the centre, and each time we did what we were told, with 'good reactions'. After each take (and I lost count of them) the dreaded cry would come from the asst. director, 'first positions please', there would be a wait varying in time from 5 to 25 minutes, and then off we would go again. The dancers in their quite heavy clothes must have lost a few pounds during the day.

The choreographer,[11] a snazzy grey-haired woman in matching grey high-heeled top boots, also harangued the dancers every now and then. From our position on the periphery it was not possible to see whether this had any effect.

A welcome relief came at 11.15 when we were given a short break for cold drinks. I remained in the quad, when I was suddenly confronted by Kate, with Toby in her arms and Dan alongside.[12] Close behind came Anne. They had been lucky enough to arrive when the road gates had been opened. I was so pleased because I wanted them to see the dancing. In spite of the tedium of doing the same thing over and over again, the sunshine and the beauty of the girls in their long dresses made up for it.

The family stood over by the porter's lodge when the crowd came back. As the asst. director had everyone on that side of the quad go in behind closed doors I was afraid that they wouldn't see anything; but I learnt later that they had been able to look through one of the windows. They couldn't fail to hear the playback, it was so strident and loud.

We broke for lunch just before 1. In order to be near the front of the queue I had changed my position to the other side of the quad. When the order of release – 'check the gates' (i.e. the camera

11 Eleanor Fazan, a distinguished British choreographer hired to find the 160 dancers and supervise the dance sequences.
12 Kate Wilson (Vivian and Anne's daughter) with her young sons Dan and Toby.

gates, to make sure that no hair or dirt had been marring the take) – came, I was thus pretty well forward, and soon had my box lunch and cup of soup in my hands. I returned to the quad early, and found Cimino, Zsigmond, and a camera crew, surrounding a camera pointed at the top of the tower. Assembled along the parapet were the members of the orchestra brass band. While the full orchestra of the playback bellowed out the 'Blue Danube', the band swayed to and fro, the stars and stripes flying above them from the flagpole, miming the music as they played. This shot didn't take long, and this camera and the others were then positioned on the terrace facing the tower and main building. One was put on a high platform at one end, another was cantilevered on timbers from an upper window; and the third was mounted on the small camera crane used last Friday. The crane could travel on the long track already built on the terrace, and it was used to good effect during the afternoon's shooting, which was still a repetition of the morning's dancing, tho' the light was now very different. Once again, take after take. Then a merciful break for tea at 4.15, set out on trestle tables along the Mansfield Road pavement.

After tea we returned for further shots of the same scene. This time the cameras had been repositioned high up on the tower and various parts of the roof, looking down on the dancers from the four quarters. The only other change in the scene that I could detect was the substitution of John Hurt's stand-in for Hurt himself. I suppose his ankle had given out after the morning's hard work. His reddish wig now adorned the head of a man very close in build and height. In the whirl of the dance it was not possible to detect the difference from where we were standing.

During the lunch break I talked with one of the professional extras. He had been a schoolmaster, and for the last four years since his retirement he had taken up this work to keep himself from being bored and to give himself some protection against inflation. He was a member of the FAA, the union which looks after extras, and had to ring them regularly to find out what work might be available.

The playback played the waltz
each time, with a deafening noise,
the 3 cameras were slowly pushed
around the tree at the centre,
and each time we did what we
were told, with 'good reactions'.
After each take (and I lost count
of them) the dreaded cry would
come from the asst. director, 'first
positions please', there would be a
wait varying in time from 5 to 25
minutes, and then off we would
go again. The dancers in their
quite heavy clothes must have lost
a few pounds during the day.

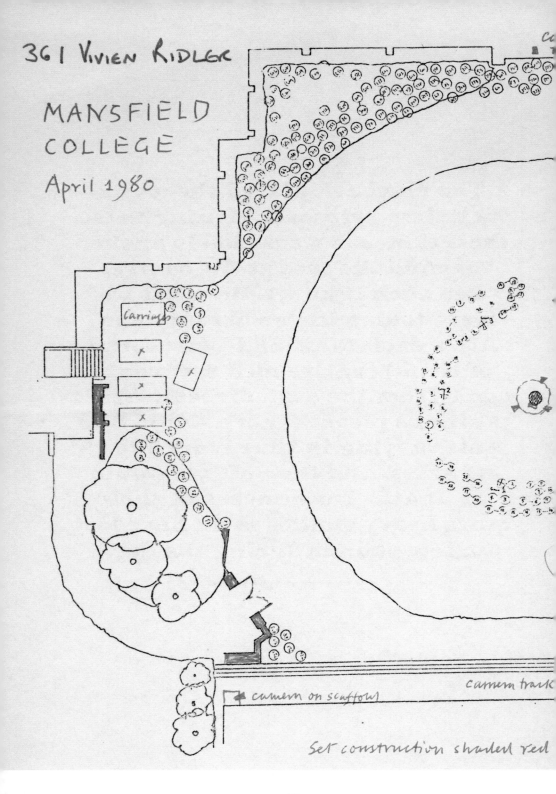

361 Vivien Ridler

MANSFIELD
COLLEGE
April 1980

Carriages

camera on scaffold

camera track

Set construction shaded red

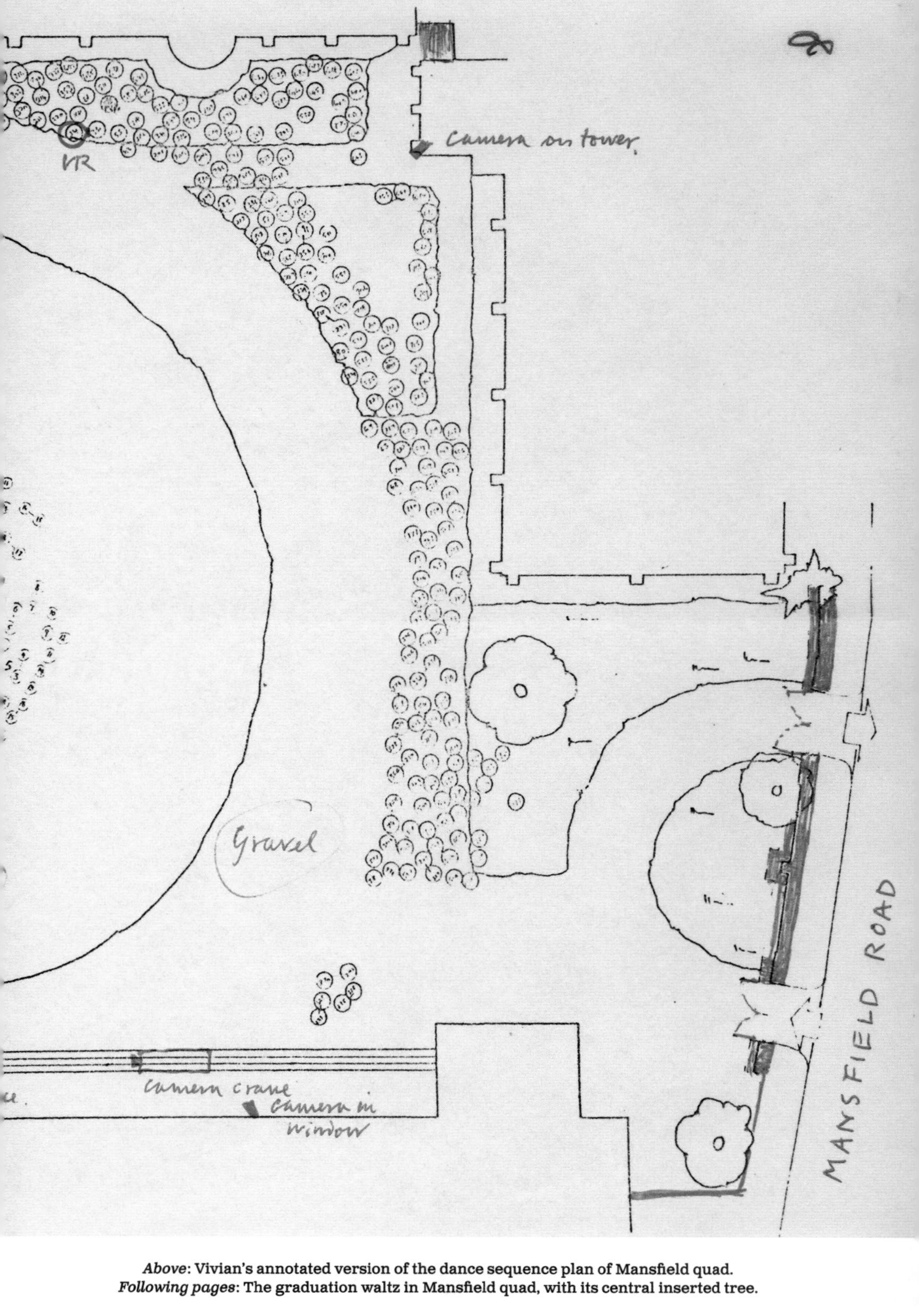
VR
Camera on tower
Gravel
Camera crane
Camera in window
MANSFIELD ROAD

Above: Vivian's annotated version of the dance sequence plan of Mansfield quad.
Following pages: The graduation waltz in Mansfield quad, with its central inserted tree.

He told me that Ray Milland, acting and directing in a film, had been the most impressive director he had worked for. Two rehearsals of each shot, two takes, finish. Then on to the next. Rather different from Cimino, tho' most of us felt that having gone to the enormous expense of setting up this scene he was entitled to cover it from every possible angle.

I forgot to mention that the women's dresses had all come from museums in the States.

After several more takes, the dancers being exhorted to show that they were really enjoying themselves, the gates were checked just before 6, and the day's work was ended. When I was paid off, back at Tent City, I was thanked and told that the services of the 'Oxford Relatives' would not be required again. I was not really sorry, but I should like to have seen the main actors being directed in some more distinctive action. I heard that Wednesday's shooting will involve a ritual fight of the students as they struggle to approach and seize the broad wreath of coloured flowers that had been placed around the tree before our afternoon's work.

Norman Pollock had not turned up on Tuesday. On Wednesday morning he rang to ask me whether I had been called. I said that I thought we had all been told last week that we would be needed, but he had been waiting for the company to call *him*, and so missed the occasion.

The film is due for release in December. It is said that the main part of the film contains 'much violence and nudity',[13] which hardly sounds like 40 million dollars' worth. Still, in spite of all the hanging around I have enjoyed the experience enormously.

---

13 Vivian writes: September 1981, 'There was, but most of the violence was the usual western "bang-bang" variety. Isabelle Huppert made a nice nude – what wasn't nice, in fact quite gratuitously unpleasant, was a prolonged and explicit rape scene in which she was the victim.' October 1981, Vivian adds: 'Alkan Allan, writing on the new BBC series, The Borgias, says "Some unkind souls are suggesting that it will turn out to be the television equivalent of Michael Cimino's Heaven's Gate, the costliest white elephant in the history of cinema. I rather hope it does, as I consider Heaven's Gate to be one of the near-masterpieces of the commercial cinema."'

Opposite: The movie's first poster, later changed (see pages 2 & 46) to emphasize the love story element.

Michael Cimino's

HEAVEN'S GATE

PARTISAN PRODUCTIONS LTD. PRESENTS

KRIS KRISTOFFERSON IN MICHAEL CIMINO'S HEAVEN'S GATE

CO-STARRING

CHRISTOPHER WALKEN, JOHN HURT, SAM WATERSTON, BRAD DOURIF

ISABELLE HUPPERT, JOSEPH COTTEN, JEFF BRIDGES
AS ELLA   AS THE REVEREND DOCTOR   ALSO STARRING

MUSIC BY   DIRECTOR OF PHOTOGRAPHY
MICHAEL CIMINO AND DAVID MANSFIELD   VILMOS ZSIGMOND, A.S.C.

PRODUCED BY   WRITTEN AND DIRECTED BY
JOANN CARELLI, MICHAEL CIMINO

T United Artists
A Transamerica Company

C O M I N G   F O R   C H R I S T M A S

ADVANCE 1 SHT. **HEAVEN'S GATE** 800112

POSTSCRIPT

September 1981

We have at last seen the film. It only lasted a week at the ABC, which is perhaps not surprising, because in its heavily-cut form it really is a mess, and in part almost incomprehensible. There are a few fine, spectacular scenes in Wyoming, and Cimino's reconstruction of a 19th-century town, with chimneys smoking and streets crowded with horses, carts, and immigrants, is impressive. But poor John Hurt's part has all but disappeared. As Barry Norman said in his cutting review of the film, he has ended up as 'The fastest draw on a hip-flask in the west.'

Isabelle Huppert is beautifully photographed, looks wonderful, and is completely miscast. Kristofferson, on the other hand, looks and seems more weighty on the screen than he did on location in Oxford.

The Oxford scenes were not as savagely cut as I had expected. Hurt's speech and capering in the Sheldonian has completely gone. I appear for about 5 seconds in the New College Lane scene where Kristofferson runs to catch up with the procession, and the dance in Mansfield is well-edited to give a feeling of pace and excitement. The film actually opens with the words 'Harvard 1870' over a shot of Tom Tower, which rather startled us. I suppose no one is supposed to recognize it. Altogether a sad result for such a vast investment of money and talent.

17 January, 1984

Dan Whistler[14] kindly invited me to see the full-length version with him at the Classic cinema in Shaftesbury Avenue in London. A friend of his, Nick Scudamore, runs the cinema and took us in

---

14 A family friend, filmmaker, and son of the glass-engraver and poet Laurence Whistler (1912-2000).

as his 'guests', which was very gracious of him. This was at the 2 p.m. performance: we saw the film with four other people.

The prologue is much extended and improved, particularly the marching and dancing. John Hurt was allowed to make his speech, not that it was comprehensible – in fact the full-length film did nothing to remove the obscurity of his part. The comical opening caption 'Harvard University 1870', printed over a shot of Tom Tower, has gone. I appear in quite a decent mid-shot in Queen's Lane, as Kristofferson dashes by. The spectacle through-out is impressive, but the prolonged and absurd violence made one feel more than ever that Cimino should have used a decent scriptwriter instead of trying to do it all himself. Not a masterpiece by any means, but the memory of some wonderful shots remains.

Rehearsal in Catte Street: left to right, John Hurt, Michael Cimino, Kris Kristofferson.

PART II

THE MOVIE
AND
ITS DIRECTOR

The only thing greater than their passion for America...
was their passion for each other.

Michael Cimino's

HEAVEN'S GATE

KRIS KRISTOFFERSON IN MICHAEL CIMINO'S HEAVEN'S GATE

CO-STARRING
CHRISTOPHER WALKEN · JOHN HURT · SAM WATERSTON · BRAD DOURIF

ISABELLE HUPPERT   JOSEPH COTTEN   ALSO STARRING
AS ELLA   AS THE REVEREND DOCTOR   JEFF BRIDGES

MUSIC BY   DIRECTOR OF PHOTOGRAPHY   PRODUCED BY   WRITTEN AND DIRECTED BY
DAVID MANSFIELD   VILMOS ZSIGMOND, A.S.C.   JOANN CARELLI   MICHAEL CIMINO

INTRODUCTION

Michael Cimino (1939–2016) led a life full of contradictions. A filmmaker who honed his craft with single-minded
determination to become a successful director, capable of
marshalling huge forces – construction workers, actors, cinema-
tographers, extras, stunt and special-effects men – in difficult
locations for shooting movies, he seems nevertheless to have felt
sufficiently insecure to have woven a web of lies about himself in
order to create an image of a brilliant, self-made visionary who
came from a tough background back East. He claimed to be younger
and taller than he actually was (he wore built-up shoes to obscure
his probable 5ft-5inch height). He claimed that his 'toxic' parents
in his home town of Westbury, Long Island, actively discouraged
his filmmaking. Yet when Charles Elton, Cimino's biographer, met
one of the surviving brothers, he described loving parents who
were proud of Michael's achievements.

Of more relevance, perhaps, in understanding the sense of
insecurity was the fact that Cimino, when he arrived in Hollywood
in 1971, was an outsider. After taking a degree in graphic design
from Michigan State University and studying fine arts at Yale –
he continued to paint throughout his life – he had made his name
as a successful director of TV commercials in New York. There he
met Joann Carelli, an agent, later his collaborator-producer, who
urged him to move to Los Angeles in order to fulfil his ambition

Opposite: Isabelle Huppert and Kris Kristofferson dominate in the main release poster, a
diminutive Christopher Walken standing at centre.

Michael Cimino and
Joann Carelli at the
Directors Guild of
America Awards
in Beverly Hills,
California, 10 March
1979, where he won
Outstanding Director
for *The Deer Hunter*.

to turn the movie scripts he was writing into projects that would
get taken on with him as director. (Carelli carried the torch for
him throughout his career, but their relationship – like so much
else in his life – was a mystery to all but themselves. They never
married, yet he treated her daughter by another man as his own.)

The new breed of young directors who were transforming
Hollywood – Martin Scorcese, Peter Bogdanovich, Francis Ford
Coppola, George Lucas, Steven Spielberg and others – came from
a different background, and were steeped in movie lore, keen
to learn from earlier pioneers such as John Ford and Howard
Hawks, and the French *nouvelle vague*. Cimino doesn't seem to
have mixed with these tyros, instead remaining something of
an isolated figure, following his own path. Nor did he cultivate

Hollywood journalists, as Coppola did relentlessly, and indeed by the time *Heaven's Gate* was in production in 1979, he had positively antagonized them by refusing them interviews, which unfortunately helped precipitate the movie's disastrous reception. (It is noteworthy that the gossipy *Easy Riders, Raging Bulls* (1998), by the journalist and former editor of *American Film* Peter Biskind, an enjoyable romp through the Hollywood of the 1970s, dwells at length on the love lives, antagonisms and films of the major directors, but includes just a few pages on Cimino, and lists only his *Heaven's Gate* in the book's Selected Filmography, unlike the full movie record given for the other big names.)

In Los Angeles Cimino devoted himself to writing numerous screenplays. Thanks to his powerful agent, Stan Kamen, he fell in with the prolific but not-quite-fashionable Clint Eastwood, finishing a script for Clint as the cop Dirty Harry in *Magnum Force,* before displaying his own undoubted chutzpah by boldly insisting that he himself should direct *Thunderbolt and Lightfoot,* based on a script he had been asked to write for the spaghetti-western star. According to Charles Elton, Eastwood decided to take a chance on the 34-year-old, telling him, 'I'll give you three days. If it doesn't work, I'll get another director.' It did work – Cimino shot the film in a tight 47 days – and *Time* magazine praised the young director's 'scrupulously controlled style', calling the 1974 picture 'one of the most ebullient and eccentric diversions around'. With its broad vistas filmed in Montana, it displayed Cimino's visual flair nurtured at Michigan and Yale.

SUCCESS WITH *THE DEER HUNTER*

Cimino had not yet 'arrived' in Hollywood. His only movie as director was seen as a Clint Eastwood film. He had to revert to his role solely as a screenwriter – though for two long years nothing he touched got made. Then his luck changed. EMI Films, the British production company, wanted to break into the US market. They asked Cimino to adapt and direct a screenplay they liked involving two soldiers playing Russian roulette for money in Vietnam. He and Deric Washburn transformed a 'buddy movie' script into something much darker, and introduced a symbolic deer-hunting scene that gave the movie its name: *The Deer Hunter*.

Displaying his considerable abilities as an organizer but also a single-minded perfectionist, over 4 months Cimino shot the film on location in 8 different US towns to represent the home town of Clairton, and in Thailand for the Vietnam sequences (700 extras took part in a night sequence in Bangkok; the Thai military were persuaded to provide vehicles, weapons and aircraft – but there were constant rumours of an imminent coup). The brilliant Hungarian-born cinematographer Vilmos Zsigmond – Oscar-winner for Spielberg's *Close Encounters of the Third Kind* (1977) – gave the movie its distinctive look with his Panavision camera for wide-screen. He had to over-develop the film to compensate for the low-light conditions in the Thai monsoon season, creating what looked like genuine grainy news footage. The stars Robert De Niro, Christopher Walken and John Savage performed all their own dangerous stunts on location – including the fall from a helicopter into a river which Cimino shot 15 times.

The alarm bells, however, began to ring for EMI and their US partner Universal, as the budget ballooned from the agreed $7.5 million to $15 million, and the film footage mounted up: it reached an extravagant 600,000 feet (about 100 hours) thanks to Cimino's multiple takes of each scene (which he claimed were necessary since the Thai footage had to be sent back to the US for processing before he could view it). Such profligacy would reach its apogee on *Heaven's Gate,* for a different hapless studio, United Artists. *The Deer Hunter,* meantime, became an unexpected hit, both at the Oscars in April 1979 (winning 5 of them) and with moviegoers, who helped it gross $48 million at the US box office. It proved to be far and away Cimino's most successful film. It has also stood the test of time. The respected film historian David Thomson, in his entry on Cimino for his authoritative *New Biographical Dictionary of Film* (2014), writes this of *The Deer Hunter*: 'Few

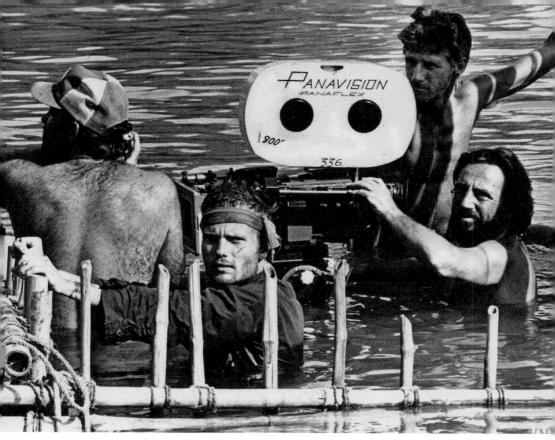

Filming *The Deer Hunter* on the River Kwai: at centre, John Savage (playing
Corporal Steven Pushkov) is seen trapped in a Vietcong bamboo cage, while
cinematographer Vilmos Zsigmond, far right, adjusts his camera. Rats
and watersnakes plagued the actors in the freezing-cold river.

movies have ever stirred audiences so powerfully. . . . I think it
is a great picture . . . to put beside *Bonnie and Clyde, King Kong,*
and *Birth of a Nation,* monuments worthy of some shame and
much exhilaration.'

By contrast, in the same book, Thomson describes Cimino's next
film, *Heaven's Gate,* as 'a disaster . . . In its making, it paraded
all the madnesses of Hollywood, and it showed how disastrous
the cult of the director had become.' As we shall see, this became
the accepted view of the movie in the US after its initial release,
hostile critical reception and commercial failure. Its stars, on
the other hand, always admired *Heaven's Gate* and its director,
a view now widely held by critics and film enthusiasts. The story
of the movie's troubled and prolonged birth is an engrossing one.

51

TURMOIL AT UNITED ARTISTS

Cimino had finally made a name for himself as a big-picture director with his Vietnam movie (incidentally pipping Coppola to the post as the first to make a successful film about that unpopular war, as he tactlessly implied – *Apocalypse Now* would finally appear one year later), but he had also gained a reputation with studios as a difficult and unhelpful director. The President of Universal said that it 'was a continuing nightmare from the day Michael finished the picture to the day we released it. That was because he was wedded to everything he shot.' Thus it is no surprise that it was to a different studio, United Artists, that Cimino turned for his next project: *The Johnson County War,* which would become *Heaven's Gate.*

United Artists had a high reputation as the maker of original, sometimes offbeat movies in its second major incarnation under Arthur Krim and Robert Benjamin, who had rescued the studio in 1951 when two of the surviving founders – Charlie Chaplin and Mary Pickford, who had established it with D W Griffith and Douglas Fairbanks in 1919 – finally gave up the struggle to keep it going. Starting with *The African Queen,* starring Humphrey Bogart, and *High Noon* with Gary Cooper, Krim and Benjamin financed and oversaw an astonishing variety of hits and quirky movies, from *Twelve Angry Men* to *Some Like It Hot,* from *West Side Story* to *Tom Jones,* from *In the Heat of the Night* to *Last Tango in Paris* – and they acquired two incredibly successful series: James Bond and the *Pink Panther* franchise with Peter Sellers. These all in turn contributed to ever-growing profits, which Krim and Benjamin understandably decided to cash in when the conglomerate Transamerica offered to buy the company in 1967, while keeping the two of them in charge of the new subsidiary. Soon, however, recession struck and profits plunged. Transamerica installed tight management systems which in due course led Krim and Benjamin to try to buy back UA. By 1978, unable to do so, they unexpectedly decamped with their top team to found a new rival studio, Orion.

Hollywood was shocked. Who at UA could now possibly replicate the movie-making magic of Krim and Benjamin? All eyes were on Transamerica and who they would appoint as new head of the studio. Andy Albeck, the man chosen as President, had been with UA for 30 years – but he was a Transamerica-type systems and figures man, not a creative.

Who would fill that role? After some vicissitudes, Albeck appointed David Field and Steven Bach as coheads of production – dismissed two decades later by Peter Biskind in his book as 'two kids with little experience'. Hardly 'kids' (Bach was 40 in 1978, and had worked at Pantheon Films before shepherding Woody Allen and others at UA), they were acutely aware of the production hole they needed to fill – while at the same time wanting to show their creative flair by signing new star directors. It was, however, unfortunate that Albeck had sprung their appointment on them unexpectedly just at the point when their UA predecessor, as a leaving present, gifted them a semi-negotiated deal with Cimino's tough agent for *The Johnson County War*. Both Field and Bach had been given an early screening of *The Deer Hunter*, which impressed them, so they perhaps too hastily concluded the deal with the agent. For, to meet the UA sales department requirement that the new film appear in time for Christmas 1979 release, in the signed contract they accepted a clause that, if Cimino went beyond the budget because of the need to shoot the movie in 69 days, he wouldn't be penalized – thus at a stroke removing all power they had to control his extravagance, financial or otherwise.

As Bach later wrote in *Final Cut* (1985), his vivid if partial account of what happened next, '*Heaven's Gate* was to be the proud centrepiece of the new administration's slate of pictures. Our *Lawrence of Arabia*, our *Doctor Zhivago*, set in the American West.'

THE JOHNSON COUNTY WAR
AND HEAVEN'S GATE

Ironically, the Krim and Benjamin regime had itself contemplated

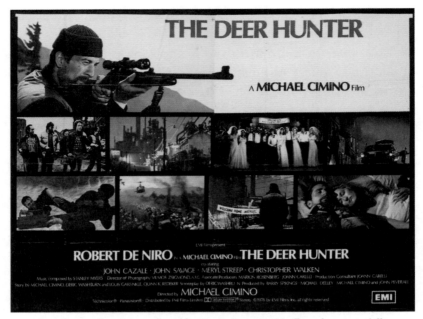

One of several posters produced for Cimino's most critically and commercially successful film, with key scenes highlighted. Compare page 104.

making a movie out of a Johnson County War script that Cimino submitted to them first in 1972, and then with adjustments and Steve McQueen's interest in 1974-76. After McQueen moved on to different projects, and other possible stars failed to materialize, UA shelved the project, while Cimino started *The Deer Hunter.*

The romance of the Old West and Wyoming (with its Johnson County) in the 1890s had an appeal for novelists and filmmakers from early on. Films as varied as *The Wild Bunch* (1969), *Butch Cassidy and the Sundance Kid* (1969) and *Little Big Man* (1970) all draw on Wyoming history, while the classic western *Shane* (1953), with Alan Ladd, is concerned with homesteading and cattle barons – the theme intrinsic to *Heaven's Gate.* The cattle barons did in reality hold immense power in Wyoming, both after 1873 when they established the Stockgrowers Association, and after 1890 when Wyoming became a US state and they controlled the state legislature. Meantime the national Homestead Act of 1862 gave homesteaders the right to claim 160 free acres of land, and hundreds of thousands moved west to do just that – conflicting with the cattle ranchers who wanted unfenced land for their steer. The ranchers decided to make an example of Johnson County, and launched an assault on the newcomers there in April 1892. However, this 'war' ended almost before it had begun, as the Buffalo townspeople had time to mount a counterattack, meaning the invaders retreated to barricade themselves into a ranch before they were indeed rescued by the cavalry, despatched by US President Harrison at the request of the Wyoming Senator (an Association member).

In the script Cimino sold to United Artists in early 1979 for the film that became *Heaven's Gate,* he made free use of genuine names from the 'war' – James Averill, Ella Watson, Nate Champion, Frank Canton, Billy Irvine and others – but often altered their actual biographies. Averill, for instance, was the local postmaster not the federal marshal, and didn't go to Harvard (though he may have attended Cornell); Ella Watson was his common-law wife, but also in reality mistress of the local bordello as the film states; Nate Champion was an Association cowboy, but probably never knew Averill or Watson; and Billy Irvine was not an Easterner and probably didn't know Averill, but he was an Association member and a power in Republican politics.

In any case, Cimino was not writing history but attempting to make a blockbuster movie on the theme of injustice and prejudice, the poor against the rich. The following sections of Part II of this book give a summary of how that worked out, through an account of the plot; a month-by-month record of the film's creation and reception; the reaction of Cimino, Zsigmond and the stars; the response of film critics to the movie; and a chronological listing and description of all Cimino's films to set *Heaven's Gate* in the context of his whole career as a director.

Film Credits for *Heaven's Gate*

Kris Kristofferson	*James Averill*
Christopher Walken	*Nathan D Champion*
John Hurt	*Billy Irvine*
Sam Waterston	*Frank Canton*
Brad Dourif	*Mr Eggleston*
Isabelle Huppert	*Ella Watson*
Joseph Cotten	*Reverend Doctor*
Jeff Bridges	*John H Bridges*
Richard Masur	*Cully*
Terry O'Quinn	*Captain Minardi*
Mickey Rourke	*Nick Ray*
Roseanne Vela	*Beautiful Girl*
Michael Cimino	Director/Screenwriter
Joann Carelli	Producer
Vilmos Zsigmond	Cinematographer
David Mansfield	Composer
Lisa Fruchtman	Editors
Gerald Greenberg	
William Reynolds	
Tom Rolf	
Partisan Productions	Production Company
United Artists	Distributor

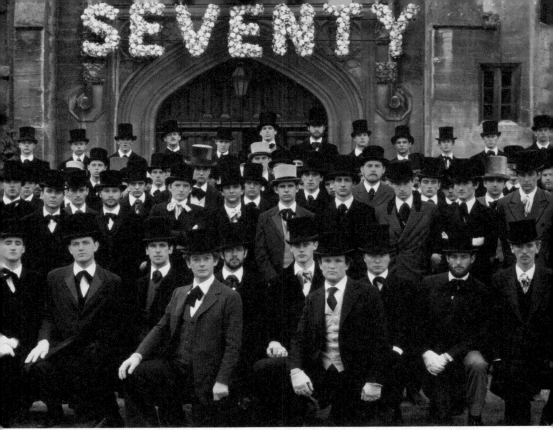

The Class of '70 lines up for a photocall, with John Hurt and Kris Kristofferson at the front.

THE PLOT

The prologue, set in 1870, focuses on two young men, Jim Averill (Kris Kristofferson) and Billy Irvine (John Hurt), who are graduating from Harvard College. During the graduation ceremony (filmed in the Sheldonian) the Dean, the Reverend Doctor (Joseph Cotten), urges the new graduates to spread culture through contact with the uncultivated. Billy Irvine, as Class of '70 orator, mocks the Dean in a facetious speech. The graduates then celebrate by dancing a waltz with their girlfriends on the Harvard green (filmed at Mansfield College), to the strains of the 'Blue Danube'. The dance culminates in a traditional rush by the graduates on a great tree at the centre of the green where Averill, full of youth and ideals (contrasting with the cynical Irvine), triumphantly retrieves a symbolic wreath of flowers.

Above: Sweetwater, the fictional town for the immigrants that Cimino's crew constructed on the edge of a lake. *Opposite*: Wallace, Idaho, was transformed into an 1889 Casper, Wyoming.

Cut to 20 years later. Averill is travelling by train out west from St Louis, bringing a fine horse and carriage for his girlfriend in Johnson County, Wyoming, where he is now federal marshal. At the end of the line in the booming town of Casper, Wyoming, Averill disembarks along with hordes of poor Eastern European immigrants. The throbbing pulse of the stationary steam locomotive adds a forbidding note behind all the noise and bustle. The local wealthy cattle farmers, formed into the Stockgrowers Association, resent the incomers as rustlers who steal their cattle. They hire gunslingers, one of whom, Nate Champion (Christopher Walken), we have already seen shoot dead an immigrant farmer who has killed a steer to feed his starving family.

Averill buys a lever-action Winchester rifle in Casper and goes to the Stockgrowers Association headquarters, a sumptuously appointed place, its atmosphere of calm contrasting with the rowdy scenes outside. Here the head of the Association, the villainous Frank Canton (Sam Waterston), is telling his members – including a drunk Billy Irvine (Averill's old Harvard friend), disturbed by Canton's speech – about plans to kill 125 named settlers as 'bandits and anarchists' for $50 a head to the gunslingers. Irvine encounters Averill and tells him of this. 'Even they can't get away with a thing like that', his friend exclaims. 'In principle everything can be done', replies Irvine. On his way out, Averill confronts Canton, who accuses him of being a traitor to his class. Averill knocks Canton to the ground.

Averill drives north to Johnson County in his horse and carriage, arriving at the main town of Sweetwater, still under construction next to a lake, with a spectacular backdrop of high mountains. He goes to the hotel where he lives, run by John Bridges (Jeff Bridges). Later he visits his girlfriend, the local madame Ella Watson (Isabelle Huppert), in her bordello where they begin to make love. They go on a wild ride in the horse and carriage, his

birthday present to her. At an enormous rink, built by Bridges, called 'Heaven's Gate', they join immigrant families and bordello girls for joyous roller-skating before dancing alone. Averill passes out drunk back at the whorehouse. We learn that Nate Champion, the Association gunslinger we have by now met several times, is also in love with Ella Watson. But he is upset that she charges him for her services, unlike Averill.

Next day, at the army fort where Averill tries unsuccessfully to obtain support in opposing the gunslingers, he is given a copy of the Association's death list. Ella Watson's name is on it. He later tells her, begging her to leave – which she won't do unless he proposes and comes with her. We glimpse a framed black-and-white photograph he has, showing him smartly dressed back East with another woman. Is he already married? Averill has a fight with Nate, who claims to know nothing about the list. Saying he has asked Ella to be his wife, Nate takes her to his cabin.

Back in Casper, the Irish station-master Cully (Richard Masur) sees the train carrying the cattlemen and gunslingers head north to Johnson County. He tries to warn Averill by telegraph, but the wires have been cut. So he rides off on horseback. Later the gunslingers – disembarked from the train outside Sweetwater – find Cully and kill him as he tries to escape.

Ella Watson leaves Nate Champion's cabin to return to her bordello, but Association men there brutally rape her, before all but one of them is shot by Averill. Nate, finally realizing his land-owner bosses want to kill Ella, goes to Canton's camp, shoots the remaining rapist, and refuses to take part in the slaughter of immigrants. Canton claims he has the backing of the US government.

When the mayor of Sweetwater tells Averill that the immigrants on the death list will be turned over to the Association, the marshal quits. Canton and the gunslingers now attack Nate Champion in his cabin. Ella tries to save him but has to flee on horseback, while the mercenaries set fire to the cabin. Nate pens a last note before dying in a hail of bullets as he comes out shooting.

Opposite: Nate Champion (Chris Walken) comes out shooting as his cabin goes up in flames.

John Bridges (Jeff Bridges) dances with Ella Watson (Isabelle Huppert) in the Sweetwater roller-skating rink called 'Heaven's Gate'. Cast and extras were sent to a training camp to learn how to roller-skate.

Back at the 'Heaven's Gate' rink the agitated settlers are roused to counterattack. Led by Ella and John Bridges, they surround Canton's camp, circling perhaps in an echo of a John Ford movie showing an American Indian attack. In the ensuing chaotic battle, filled with dust and gunsmoke, the drunken Association man Billy Irvine, sensing defeat, reminisces about Paris but is shot dead by Ella. Canton escapes to get help. Both sides withdraw temporarily.

Ella and Averill find Nate Champion's corpse at his charred cabin, with a note: 'Goodbye Ella and Jim, if I never see you again.' Averill now decides to help the immigrants. Using his classical training at Harvard, he adopts a Roman plan of attack. With logs and remnants of their horse-drawn carts the immigrants besiege the Association camp, gradually moving in with their wheeled barricades which afford some protection from gunfire. Sticks of dynamite blow holes in the camp defences. Just as it seems the immigrants are about to win, Canton arrives with the US cavalry, who stop the fighting and rescue the remaining mercenaries. Hundreds of dead bodies and dead horses litter the scene, like a Civil War battlefield.

At John Bridge's cabin, Ella and Averill prepare to leave for good, but are ambushed by Canton and some Association men. In the ensuing gunfight, Canton and Bridges are both killed; Ella dies too, and Averill weeps as he holds her in his arms.

In the epilogue, set a decade or so later in 1903, we find an older-looking Averill, smartly dressed in a sailing outfit, watching a sunset from the deck of his steam yacht anchored off Newport, Rhode Island. He has resumed the life of ease and privilege as an Easterner he had idealistically abandoned to go West three decades before. He goes below, where a beautiful middle-aged woman in a white dress lies asleep on a sofa. She must be the woman shown in the framed photograph on the table here (repeatedly shown earlier too), the girl he danced with at the Harvard graduation 30 years before. She wakes and asks for a cigarette. In silence Averill complies, lights it and – face quivering with emotion – returns to the deck, where he stares at the water as the story ends.

The final showdown between the attacking settlers and the besieged Association men.

. . . they surround Canton's camp,
circling perhaps in an echo of
a John Ford movie showing an
American Indian attack. In the
ensuing chaotic battle, filled with
dust and gunsmoke, the drunken
Association man Billy Irvine . . .
is shot dead by Ella.

Michael Cimino's HEAVEN'S GATE

KRIS KRISTOFFERSON IN MICHAEL CIMINO'S HEAVEN'S GATE

CO-STARRING
CHRISTOPHER WALKEN   JOHN HURT   SAM WATERSTON   BRAD DOURIF

ALSO STARRING
ISABELLE HUPPERT   JOSEPH COTTEN   JEFF BRIDGES

MUSIC BY
DAVID MANSFIELD
AS ELLA

DIRECTOR OF PHOTOGRAPHY
VILMOS ZSIGMOND, A.S.C.
AS THE REVEREND DOCTOR

PRODUCED BY
JOANN CARELLI

WRITTEN AND DIRECTED BY
MICHAEL CIMINO

70mm Six-Track

□□ DOLBY STEREO ™
IN SELECTED THEATRES

TECHNICOLOR®

ORIGINAL MOTION PICTURE SOUNDTRACK
ON LIBERTY RECORDS AND TAPES

T⊤ **United Artists**
A Transamerica Company

1 SHT. INT'L STYLE B

THE MAKING AND UNMAKING
OF *HEAVEN'S GATE*: A CHRONOLOGY

1971 Cimino drafts a script for *The Johnson County War* which a producer shows to 20th Century Fox, who turn it down in 1972, as does United Artists the same year. UA's reader dislikes the 'mayhem/murder', but the main reason for the rejection is the fact that Cimino has yet to direct a movie.

1974 With the success of Cimino's directorial debut, *Thunderbolt and Lightfoot* (see p.103), and Steve McQueen's interest in *The Johnson County War* script, United Artists does a deal with Cimino for the movie, on the basis that either McQueen and his new bride Ali McGraw, or some other named stars will be signed up.

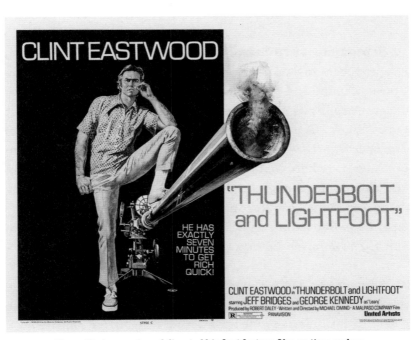

Above: Cimino wrote and directed his first feature film on time and on budget for his demanding sponsor, Eastwood. *Opposite*: This poster seeks to emphasize both the main love triangle and the epic last battle.

1975–76 No stars have joined the project (John Wayne has even been suggested to play Jim Averill), nor has a change of title to *Paydirt* helped – so the movie is shelved at UA, while Cimino moves on to *The Deer Hunter* (see pp 103-105).

January 1978 Unable to buy back United Artists from conglomerate Transamerica that had acquired it in 1967, UA's top management team of Arthur Krim and Robert Benjamin unexpectedly decides to leave to set up a rival studio, Orion. Krim and Benjamin have become famous in Hollywood for rescuing United Artists in 1951 and as truly independent producers making such original hits as *High Noon, Some Like It Hot, West Side Story* and many others. So their departure causes consternation in the movie business. Who will replace these geniuses?

When Transamerica appoints Andy Albeck – a UA stalwart for 30 years, but a numbers and systems man, not a movie-maker – as UA President, Hollywood asks: where is the creative talent?

17 September 1978 Steven Bach – one of the New York-based UA producers tasked with revitalizing the forward programme – meets Cimino and Joann Carelli, the director's collaborator-producer. Carelli has already given Bach, together with his West Coast fellow UA producer David Field, an advance screening of *The Deer Hunter,* which impresses them both. Now, over lunch in Los Angeles (where Cimino lives), Bach gets to know the director, and likes him – though thinks he perhaps resembles a 'slightly pampered Roman senator', a short, stocky man. At the end of the meal he is handed a script for the movie Cimino now wants to make: *The Johnson County War.*

25 September 1978 David Field and Steven Bach are made coheads of production at United Artists. The same day they agree a deal with Cimino's tough agent, Stan Kamen, for *The Johnson County War* (which 4 months later has a new title, making it sound less like an unfashionable western: *Heaven's Gate*). The budget is

$7.8 million, to include $500,000 for Cimino, $100,000 for Carelli, and $850,000 for the male lead Kris Kristofferson. Thus, as Bach ruefully reflects later in his book *Final Cut*, 'our first official act . . . had been to make the deal that would destroy the company'.

Late February 1979 At a fraught meeting in Paris, Field and Bach are manoeuvred by Cimino into accepting the virtually unknown and to them highly unsuitable Isabelle Huppert as the film's leading lady, Ella Watson. The two UA producers learn how stubborn and difficult Cimino can be, while Cimino now knows he can get his own way.

Early April 1979 Contract signed, with a revised budget of $11.5 million for a 69-day shoot. Cimino, via his agent, has won the extraordinary provision that 'any and all monies in excess of the approved cash budget expended . . . to complete the picture in time for a Christmas 1979 release date shall not be treated as overbudget', thus removing virtually all power UA has to limit expenditure.

10 April 1979 Cimino's *The Deer Hunter* wins 5 Oscars at the Academy Awards, including Best Picture (announced at the ceremony by John Wayne) and Best Director (the Oscar ironically being handed to Cimino by Francis Ford Coppola, whose own Vietnam movie is years late).

11 April 1979 At a monthly UA production meeting in Los Angeles, in the presence of Transamerica Chairman Jim Harvey and UA President Danny Albeck, UA's highly experienced senior production accountant, Lee Katz, gives his firm opinion that the budget is suspect and that the picture will probably cost $15 million, assuming the 69-day target for completion of filming is met (which he doubts it will be).

16 April 1979 Filming starts near the small town of Kalispell, Montana, on the edge of Glacier National Park in the Rocky

The expensive locomotive filmed bringing immigrants and Jim Averill
(Kris Kristofferson) out West created a dramatic spectacle early on in the movie.

———————

A historic train costing $150,000 to transport (comparable to the entire fee for a leading lady in a movie at this time) is brought here from Colorado for the shoot.

———————

Mountains near the US border with Canada. A construction crew of hundreds has been based here already for 3 months, building the fictional town of Sweetwater to the north, delayed by avalanches that render access roads impassable. The town of Wallace, Idaho, 3 hours' drive away, is transformed into the 1889 town of Casper, Wyoming. A historic train costing $150,000 to transport (comparable to the entire fee for a leading lady in a movie at this time) is brought here from Colorado for the shoot. Cast costumes are meticulously copied from thousands of historic photographs.

End April 1979 After only 2 weeks of filming, over $5 million has already been spent. Cimino often does 30 takes of a single scene. UA's Field goes to Kalispell to try to get Cimino to speed up, but is rebuffed.

Field and Bach are simultaneously having to oversee some 50 other UA projects at various stages of development.

End May 1979 With costs rising at over $1 million a week, a junior UA executive with production experience, Derek Kavanagh, is sent to Montana and works out that at the current rate of progress the filming will be completed by 3 January 1980 (instead of the end June 1979 needed for a Christmas release). Cimino refuses to speak to him or allow him on set.

1 June 1979 By now *Heaven's Gate* has already cost $10 million, with three-quarters of the script still to be shot. Moreover, film crew and extras are mostly being paid at overtime rates, thanks to Cimino's takes, retakes and more retakes, and the training camp to which they are sent to learn everything from horse-riding and shooting to roller-skating and cock-fighting. (The settlers of the Old West really did roller-skate for pleasure.) One scene, involving Kristofferson lashing out with a whip at those trying to wake him from a drunken stupor, requires 52 takes and a whole day's shooting.

UA's President Albeck calculates that with promotional and

interest costs added he could end up having to finance a $50-million movie – an unheard-of sum for his company, equivalent to half that year's total budget for *all* UA productions. *Is the movie any good?*, he and his executives want to know. *Will it be a box-office success?*

6 June 1979 Field and Bach fly in to Kalispell. They witness Cimino storm off after his collaborator and producer, Carelli, unsuccessfully tries to dissuade him from his scheme to install an irrigation system in a 156-acre field they later discover he has bought for the final battle sequence, where he wants lush grass as a contrast to the subsequent bloody quagmire. But the director does show 30 minutes of footage, which impresses them with 'the poetry of America' (shots taken before sunset). They also admire the actors' performances. Kristofferson holds the screen, 'at moments recalling Gary Cooper'; Walken looks 'haunted, dangerous'; while Huppert, to their amazement, they experience as 'incandescent . . . glowing in the lamplight'.

Bach reports back positively to Albeck, 'It looks like David Lean decided to make a western.' Nevertheless, with Cimino threatening to take his masterpiece to another studio if they don't back him fully, they decide to call his bluff – alarmed anyway at the astronomical costs – and subsequently approach Warner Bros, 20th Century Fox and EMI as possible partners. EMI is initially interested, but in the end says no. Word may now get about that the movie is in trouble.

1 August 1979 With Field away on honeymoon, Bach returns to Kalispell supported by the heavyweight presence of Dean Stolber, lawyer and UA's head of business affairs. Cimino's agent – keen to save the director from himself – has told Bach that the only thing he will understand is force. 'Hit him hard.'

The UA duo present an ultimatum: a total budget of $25 million ($16 million has already been spent), 45 more days to complete the filming, Cimino to have final cut *if* the movie runs to 3 hours or under – and no prologue and epilogue (a gambit on UA's part).

Back to the wall, Cimino says he *can* speed up – as, he tells them unexpectedly, he did for Clint Eastwood on *Thunderbolt and Lightfoot* (see p.103; Eastwood generally wanted scenes shot with only 2 or 3 takes).

5 August 1979 Field delivers a document confirming UA's legal takeover of production, with a more attainable budget of $27.5 million which, if kept to in Montana, will rise to $30 million so as to include prologue, epilogue and postproduction work. Cimino must agree, or resign. He agrees.

10 August 1979 Todd McCarthy in the Hollywood magazine *Daily Variety* reveals the new $30-million figure. He has heard that John Hurt (Billy Irvine in the movie) is fuming because he has been kept there in Montana with virtually no work until he gets killed in the final battle much later on. Whatever happens, Hurt says, he will go to England by 15 October for another film.

'The cat is out of the bag' on *Heaven's Gate's* troubled production, as UA's publicist puts it. And he has 'no stills, no production information, no cooperation, no interviews, no nothing' from the secretive and uncooperative Cimino with which to promote a counterstory.

26 August & 2 September 1979 The *Los Angeles Times* publishes two articles, the first full of spiteful remarks about the dead hand of the 'accountants' now in charge at UA – made by members of the former regime who have set up the rival studio, Orion; the second headlined 'An Unauthorized Progress Report on *Heaven's Gate*': a freelance writer called Lee Gapay, refused an interview in Kalispell about the picture, had signed on as an extra for 2 months and written up an exposé. The extras, he reported, were being badly treated – injured (16 on one day), forced to wallow in mud, swelter in heat and inhale toxic dust and smoke. Work might begin at 7.30 a.m. with lunch only at 4.30 p.m. Cimino had splurged $10,000 on a jeep and bought 156 acres of land. The story is sold to newspapers and media outlets across America, starved as they are of news about the picture from UA or the production team out in Montana.

3 September 1979 *Time* magazine runs an article by James Willwerth entitled 'The Making of Apocalypse Next' (an allusion to the much-delayed, 3-year production and vast overspend on Coppola's *Apocalypse Now*, just being released finally by UA). The production is referred to as 'History's Most Expensive Footnote'. David Field – who had authorized Willwerth's trip to Kalispell – is quoted as saying, 'I think Michael is making a masterpiece.'

2 October 1979 End of Montana shoot after a final 4 weeks of filming the climactic battle between the mercenaries and immigrants. All the actors have been woken each day at 3.30 a.m. and driven for 3 hours along dirt roads to the battle site. It has involved almost all principal cast members, hundreds of extras and crew and stunt and special-effects men, hundreds of wagons, thousands of explosions – and scores of horses whose welfare becomes a major issue of contention long after the event. Jeff Bridges years later comments: 'Even in a real battle you don't do it over and over again.'

In total, Cimino has printed 1.3 million feet of film (220 hours) which, simply to view, would take 10 days – and will take a year to edit and create a fully finished print.

14 December 1979 The original date scheduled by United Artists for the premiere – which eventually takes place a year later.

11 March 1980 David Field unexpectedly announces his departure for 20th Century Fox. Although he has just personally won from Albeck agreement that Cimino *can* film his prologue and epilogue, he chafes at having to take all decisions with Bach, cohead of production at UA. Decades later he says he regrets abandoning the movie.

17 March 1980 Cimino flies to England to prepare for filming the 'Harvard' prologue in Oxford.

19 March 1980 After his proposed prologue budget of $5.2 million is turned down, Cimino uncharacteristically agrees to a lower figure of $3 million.

26 March 1980 Costume fitting for extras at Pinewood Studio.

9 April 1980 Filming takes place in the Sheldonian, hired by Cimino for £10,000 per day, and lasts well into the evening.

11 April 1980 Scenes shot in Catte Street, New College Lane and Queen's Lane as a procession with a brass band (playing 'When the Saints Go Marching In') and students makes its way towards the Sheldonian. Vivian is picked by Cimino to stand with his foot on a carriage step in Queen's Lane as Kristofferson rushes past to catch up with the procession.

15 April 1980 Filming takes place at Mansfield College, where a tree has been winched in and fixed into the centre of the quad round which dancers, choreographed by Eleanor Fazan, perform a waltz to the sound of the 'Blue Danube' (chosen by Cimino as a near-contemporary composition that would have been somewhat risqué in 1870).

26 June 1980 Cimino finally gives United Artists' bosses their first screening of the complete film, having worked 18-hour days for 8 months to edit it with his assistant Penny Shaw. It lasts a staggering 5 hours and 25 minutes (325 minutes). They insist it be cut.

October 1980 By now Cimino, and 3 editors, have reduced the running time to 3 hours 39 minutes (219 minutes).

18 November 1980 Premiere in New York, without anyone at UA having seen the finished film. It is a disaster. Isabelle Huppert recalls later that half the audience leave at the intermission.

19 November 1980 The press reviews are uniformly damning – probably the worst ever for a first night – exacerbated by Cimino's bad relations with the media. In a panic, he insists that the nationwide release is postponed so that he can produce a shortened version. His letter to the head of United Artists, agreed in advance by them and published on 24 November, states:

'It is painfully obvious to me that the pressures of the schedule and the missing crucial step of public previews clouded my perception of the film. . . . I am asking you to withdraw the film from distribution temporarily to allow me to present to the public a film finished with the same care and thoughtfulness with which we began it.'

The debacle moves the story from the arts pages to press front pages, making the film a laughing stock.

Early February 1981 The results of 'secretly' previewing a heavily cut version of the film (2 hours 29 minutes or 149 minutes) in six cities far from New York and Hollywood are inconclusive: audiences neither love nor hate the movie.

21 April 1981 The cut film is released in 810 movie theatres nationwide. It is a miserable failure and closes after 2 weeks. It grosses only $3.5 million to set against the $44 million production and promotion cost.

May 1981 United Artists is sold by Transamerica to Kirk Kerkorian, owner of the MGM studio, for $383 million (having been bought in 1967 for $180 million). UA remains profitable ($22 million) even after the failure of *Heaven's Gate*, but the debacle helps make Transamerica receptive to Kerkorian's highly attractive offer.

Isabelle Huppert, Jeff Bridges and Michael Cimino wait anxiously for audience reaction at the press preview on 18 November 1980.

Premiere in New York, without anyone at UA having seen the finished film. It is a disaster. Isabelle Huppert recalls later that half the audience leave at the intermission.

On 20 May the cut version is entered by UA at the Cannes Film Festival, but fails to win any prizes or popularity with audiences. Instead it is the sale of UA to MGM that makes the headlines.

Autumn 1983 The full version is screened in London to a generally favourable critical reception, but lasts no more than a few months before disappearing from circulation again.

The failure of the film comes to be seen as the defining moment in the demise of the power of the auteur-director that had characterized the 1970s. Martin Scorcese – whose masterpiece *Raging Bull* was favourite to win the 1981 Oscar for Best Picture but lost out to Robert Redford's old-fashioned *Ordinary People* – says, '*Heaven's Gate* undercut us all. I knew at the time that something had died.' Francis Ford Coppola – of *The Godfather* (1972) and *Apocalypse Now* (1979) fame – also blames Cimino, even though his own *One from the Heart* of 1980 had been a comparable catastrophe. With expensive sets, including a whole airport, its costs had risen from $15 million to $26 million, yet it grossed a mere $700,000 – even less than *Heaven's Gate*.

As the studio producer Peter Bart says (Biskind, *Easy Riders, Raging Bulls,* p. 406), 'At the beginning of the decade, you have a group of people who really wanted to be on budget and on schedule. They were earnest young people who couldn't believe . . . that the studios would be able to accommodate them. By the end of the decade, they became the big exploiters of the system.' With the staggering success of upbeat escapist fantasies like *Star Wars* (1977, production cost $11 million, US box office $775 million, plus endless merchandise) and its 7 sequels, in the 1980s the studios turn away from the auteur-directors with their often downbeat messages.

20 November 2012 MGM, by now long since the owner of the distribution rights after its takeover of United Artists in 1981, releases a 3 hour 36 minute (216 minute) 'Director's Cut' version on Blu-ray disc and DVD. This has been supervised by Cimino

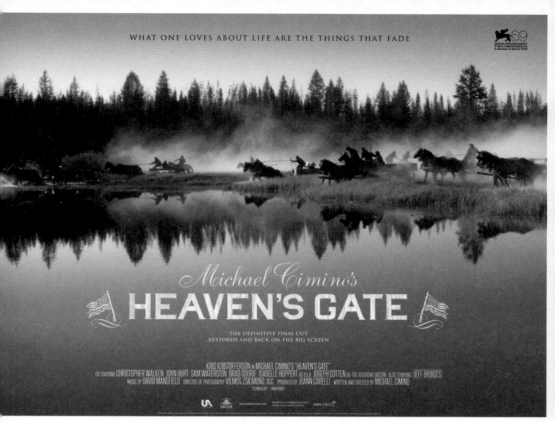

WHAT ONE LOVES ABOUT LIFE ARE THE THINGS THAT FADE

Michael Cimino's
HEAVEN'S GATE

THE DEFINITIVE FINAL CUT
RESTORED AND BACK ON THE BIG SCREEN

KRIS KRISTOFFERSON IN MICHAEL CIMINO'S "HEAVEN'S GATE"
CO-STARRING CHRISTOPHER WALKEN JOHN HURT SAM WATERSTON BRAD DOURIF ISABELLE HUPPERT AS ELLA JOSEPH COTTEN AS THE REVEREND DOCTOR ALSO STARRING JEFF BRIDGES
MUSIC BY DAVID MANSFIELD DIRECTOR OF PHOTOGRAPHY VILMOS ZSIGMOND, ASC PRODUCED BY JOANN CARELLI WRITTEN AND DIRECTED BY MICHAEL CIMINO
TECHNICOLOR® PANAVISION®

Promotional image for the 'definitive final cut' version of the movie,
approved by Cimino and reissued by MGM in 2012.

and Carelli, and is his preferred version of the film. He had not
seen the film for more than 30 years, so painful had its original
rejection been. Now he has taken the decision to remove the sepia
tint he and Zsigmond had used to convey an antique look – and
which viewers complained seemingly shrouded the movie in cigar
smoke. The result is a revelation, with lush green landscapes and
snow-white mountains.

After a screening in New York, Cimino and the movie get a
standing ovation. Kristofferson says, 'It was a catastrophe for
both our careers, but worth it.' Critics widely praise it as a flawed
masterpiece.

28, 29, or 30 June 2016 (the exact date is unknown) Cimino
dies alone in his house in Los Angeles, aged 77.

79

CIMINO, ZSIGMOND AND THE STARS
ON *HEAVEN'S GATE*

Michael Cimino

Cimino's training in graphic design at Michigan State University and fine arts at Yale helped develop his strong and original visual sense – for which he was always admired – as comes out in his interview with George Hickenlooper. But his self-confidence and prestige took so great a knock from the disastrous reception of Heaven's Gate *that his career and movie-making abilities never fully recovered.*

[Zsigmond and I] wanted to give people . . . the same kind of vitality that was in all the pictures we looked through of the real West. . . . One is used to very bleak landscapes and sparsely peopled towns, and the photographs of the period communicate such a different image. We wanted this incredible bustling activity and this explosion of energy, and a sense of something about to be born.'
(Quoted in George Hickenlooper, *Reel Conversations*, Citadel Press 1991, p.86)

'I like to work with floorplans, rather than storyboards. . . . I begin to lay out my shots . . . based on catching the choreography of movement that happens in the rehearsal process. If we have a battle scene or a scene that involves dancing, . . . my tendency is to . . . work those things out so that they happen in real time. For example, the waltz or the roller-skating sequences in *Heaven's Gate*, they are choreographed to happen in the amount of time that is on the screen. . . . It gives me the opportunity to cover the same event in an almost documentary manner. You can combine the large, formal compositions with

a very free, very loose component of cameras.'
(Hickenlooper 1991, pp 81-82)

'I think that most of the people who made the movie have never broken faith with it . . . neither I nor the producer, nor the actors, nor the crew has regretted making the movie. . . There was no time for previews. There was great pressure from inside United Artists to get it out. I expected that it would open at two small cinemas in New York and LA, and that I would be able to change things, like Kubrick did with *2001*. But it was made into a conspicuous event.'

'One of the things that is disturbing about that sort of [negative] reaction has to do with all your colleagues. For instance, David Mansfield, who wrote all the music. . . . It was his first time and it was a superior score.'

'Vittorio Storaro, who photographed *Reds*, said to Vilmos Zsigmond . . . that he thought Vilmos was bound to take the Oscar for *Heaven's Gate*, but you do not like to see your own people not getting work.'
(Interview, *The Times*, 12 August 1983)

'At least in the old days, when they lashed you to a post and whipped you, they stopped once you'd passed out.'
(Quoted in Jean Vallely, 'The Opening and Closing of Heaven's Gate,' *Rolling Stone*, 5 February 1981)

'When John Kennedy was assassinated, a lot of people felt better. Because he was so brilliant he gave them bad consciences about their own lives. I don't compare myself to Kennedy, of course. But certain journalists have been waiting to destroy me for similar reasons. Because I represent success and talent.'
(As reported defending himself and the film at the Cannes Film Festival, May 1981)

'It's one of the things that movies do offer you, despite all their hardships – they offer you moments of transcendence. We all want to experience that in our lives, a moment when we're two feet off the ground . . . What other reason is there? Michelangelo spent a couple of years on his back with paint dropping into his eyes while some crazy pope was off fighting wars. What else was he doing it for?'

('Michael Cimino Revisits His Notorious Flop *Heaven's Gate***, Which Maybe was a Masterpiece All Along', www.villagevoice. com/2013-03-20)**

Vilmos Zsigmond

Zsigmond (1930-2016) was one of the two Hungarian-born cin- ematographers responsible for the distinctive look of the best Hollywood movies of the 1970s. He won an Oscar for Spielberg's Close Encounters of the Third Kind *(1977), and worked with Robert Altman, John Boorman, Brian De Palma and Woody Allen as well. For him, mood was more important than beauty, realism created with simple lighting, shot with a wide-screen Panavision camera. His Oscar-nominated cinematography for Cimino's* The Deer Hunter *(1978) was widely admired, though he later fell out with Cimino, believing he was taking too much credit on that movie's look. However, Zsigmond shared the blame with the director for the smoky, yellowish tinge created for* Heaven's Gate *– intended to replicate old sepia photographs, but criticized for obscuring the action.*

'I like to be on a picture at least four weeks before it starts, talking to the director, watching rehearsals, thinking. Then I can come up with ideas – how to light it, what kind of mood I want to build. The most important thing for a cameraman to know is the kind of story the director wants to tell. Then visually, with my lighting and mood, I underline what he is trying to say.'

'Today in movie-making you have to be very economical. We don't have all the time to shoot. We had lots of time on *Heaven's Gate*, then United Artists cut off all the money, which meant we couldn't fool around anymore. If you spend three hours on the lighting, it had better be on the screen.'

('Vilmos Zsigmond: Hot Shot with a Camera', www.rollingstone.com/ movie/news)

'I'm sure that once it becomes known that . . . [the prologue] was shot in this way [ie a tight schedule], people will question why we spend ten million dollars on a film when it can be done for two million dollars. . . . We did it because we were pushed to do it, but I feel that directors and cameramen should have the luxury of shooting schedules that give them room to think a little bit, to create. I don't believe this is the way to shoot important sequences – but we did it.'

(Vilmos Zsigmond, 'Behind the Cameras on *Heaven's Gate*', *American Cinematographer*, 1980)

Kris Kristofferson

Kristofferson (Jim Averill in the movie) was a renowned country music composer and singer in the 1970s and later, as well as a star in three Sam Peckinpah films, including Pat Garrett and Billy the Kid *(1973), Martin Scorcese's* Alice Doesn't Live Here Anymore *(1974), and the romantic drama* A Star is Born *(1976) with Barbra Streisand, for which he received a Golden Globe Best Actor Award. Although the failure of* Heaven's Gate *at the box office and with the critics affected his A-list Hollywood status, he continued making movies for two further decades and carried on with his successful singer-songwriting life – he was inducted into the Country Music Hall of Fame in 2004. He admired Cimino's vision, and remained loyal to what the director had been trying to achieve right up to the reissue of their controversial movie in 2012.*

BEFORE THE PREMIERE: 'I've never seen a film where not just the actors but the whole crew have become so involved . . . They call him the Ayatollah Cimino . . . He's totally committed to the film. Sometimes we were working eighteen hours a day in Montana. After the rest of us had gone to bed, Michael would stay up and watch the rushes. This was for six months. I don't know when he slept. . . .He seems to sense intuitively exactly how an actor feels. . . .

He would get an idea for someone's performance and spontaneously magnify that character. . . . Cimino really hasn't got a director's ego. Whatever it cost was in film . . . It's probably the best film that I'll ever be in.'

(Interview, *Isis* [Oxford student magazine], Spring 1980)

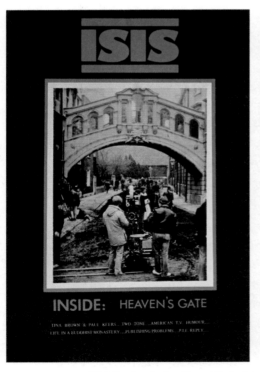

Nick Kent – who has himself had a later prominent career as a filmmaker and was an extra in *Heaven's Gate* – wrote an article about the shooting of the Oxford scenes for the student magazine *Isis* in 1980.

'Chris Walken told me he would trust Michael implicitly, so that's the way I went at it. Just do whatever this artist is trying to get done. I just figured it was his creative eye, and I trusted it.'

(Quoted in Michael Bonner, 'Michael Cimino Remembered,' *Uncut*, 4 July 2016)

AFTER THE PREMIERE: 'My manager got Alzheimer's disease and my agent died and my family split apart and then ... the film was blown out of the water. . . . [Michael] was trying to make a real piece of art, and he was fightin' the philistines the whole fuckin' way.'

(Interview, *The Independent*, June 1996)

Christopher Walken

Walken (Nate Champion) has appeared in over 100 movies, including Annie Hall *(1977),* Pennies from Heaven *(1981), as a Bond villain in* A View to a Kill *(1985),* Batman Returns *(1992), and* Pulp Fiction *(1994). He plays the young Pennsylvania steelworker Nick in Cimino's* The Deer Hunter *(1978), for which he won an Academy Award as Best Supporting Actor. To prepare for Nick's necessary gaunt appearance later on in the film, he consumed only bananas, rice and water for a week.*

'Well, I don't play heroes . . . I never played the guy who gets the girl.'

(Interview, *The Palm Beach Post*, 29 October 2004)

'I always thought [*Heaven's Gate*] was good and never really understood the beating it took at the time. . . . It always seemed extreme. It certainly was always a beautiful movie to look at. Often things are not as bad as they are touted to be and also not as good as they are touted to be.'

(Interview, *IndieWire*, 13 December 2012)

Isabelle Huppert

Regarded today as 'one of the best actresses in the world', with innumerable awards and over 120 films to her name, Huppert was cast as Ella Watson by Cimino in Heaven's Gate, *her first English-language movie, against strong opposition from United Artists, who wanted a star known to US audiences. She has worked with directors ranging from Claude Chabrol, Jean-Luc Godard and Andrzej Wajda to Otto Preminger and Joseph Losey, displaying her versatility. Her performance in Paul Verhoeven's* Elle *(2016) earned her a Golden Globe Award and an Oscar nomination as Best Actress.*

'A very impressive film, and probably one of the most memorable professional adventures I ever had in my life.'
(Interview, *The Independent*, 31 August 1995)

'It's very hard to refuse something with Michael. I'm afraid of horses and I can't dance very well. I can't do anything I do in this movie.' Cimino replied, 'When you ask a great actress to do something impossible, she just does it.'
(Sandy Gillet, 'Michael Cimino – Paris Master Class,' *EcranLarge* website, 20 July 2005)

'I loved him. He was extraordinary . . . until he passed away recently, one of the greatest living American filmmakers.

'He had an amazing ability to go from the immensely big to tiny intimacy. . . . I always thought it was a masterpiece. Now everyone reckons it is a great, great film.'
(Online interview soon after Cimino's death in 2016, LMU School of Film & Television)

John Hurt

Classically trained in the theatre and blessed with a much-loved gravelly voice, Hurt (1940-2017) was one of the great postwar

British actors. He appeared in a huge variety of films over five decades, but his peak came with Midnight Express *(1978), winning him Golden Globe and BAFTA awards,* Alien *(1979), where a hideous creature explodes from his stomach,* The Elephant Man *(1980), and* Heaven's Gate. *Here he plays Kristofferson's Harvard friend William Irvine in the prologue, who becomes inebriated and disenchanted later as an Association cattle baron in Wyoming.*

'I suppose that he is an increasing alcoholic's view of the lunacy of human behaviour – really much too similar to myself to be an easy role to play.'

'[Cimino] is an extremely complex little Napoleon.'
(Interview, *Isis***, Spring 1980)**

Jeff Bridges

Winner of an Academy Award for Best Actor as an alcoholic singer in Crazy Heart *(2009), Bridges has appeared in over 75 feature films, 6 of them gaining him an Oscar nomination – including Cimino's* Thunderbolt and Lightfoot *(1974) (see p.103). While acting the part of John Bridges in* Heaven's Gate, *he often played guitar with singer-songwriter Kristofferson between takes. He later himself released 3 studio albums.*

'The many months of shooting in Montana were one-of-a-kind movie-making experience. When *Heaven's Gate* came out, many critics called it a flop, a disaster. Well . . . that's just their opinion. To me, and many others, it's a masterpiece, and grows in beauty each time it's seen.'

'Michael Cimino was a splendid filmmaker. Getting to work with him was a great pleasure and honor, and a real stroke of luck, a blessing.'
(From Bridges' Facebook post in 2016, after Cimino's death that year)

THE CRITICS ON *HEAVEN'S GATE*

AFTER THE NEW YORK PREMIERE ON 18 NOVEMBER 1980
The lacerating reviews in the American press on the original long version of the movie led to its immediate withdrawal so that a shortened version could be released nationwide in 1981.

'*Heaven's Gate* fails so completely that you might suspect that Mr Cimino sold his soul to the Devil to obtain the success of *The Deer Hunter* and the Devil has just come around to collect.

'The grandeur of vision of the Vietnam film has turned pretentious. The feeling for character has vanished and Mr Cimino's approach to his subject is so predictable that watching the movie is like a forced, four-hour walking tour of one's own living room.'

'*Heaven's Gate* is something quite rare these days – an unqualified disaster.'

(Vincent Canby, *The New York Times*, 19 November 1980, a review that became news itself, quoted in *Time, Newsweek, Screen International* and on TV networks)

'I am a little surprised that many of the same critics who lionized Cimino for *The Deer Hunter* have now thrown him to the wolves with equal enthusiasm. I was never taken in. . . . Hence, the stupidity and incoherence of *Heaven's Gate* came as no surprise since very much the same stupidity and incoherence had been amply evident in *The Deer Hunter*.'

(Andrew Sarris, *The Village Voice*)

'Since there was no end to the talk of his genius back in *The Deer Hunter* days, many of us who saw that film for the dreck that it was are heartily enjoying ourselves as his former admirers eat their words.'

(*Films in Review*)

'The amount of revisionism at work regarding *The Deer Hunter* would make any good Stalinist proud. The critics seem to have used *Heaven's Gate* as a way to rereview *The Deer Hunter*, and to point out that they never really liked it.'

(Jean Vallely, *Rolling Stone*)

'The *Heaven's Gate* fiasco caused almost as much joy as dismay. [The blame can be divided between Cimino], who has been vain, foolish and wasteful beyond belief, and an inept leadership at United Artists – a group of men who apparently cannot read a script, who lack the confidence to act on their intuitions and doubts, and who watched Cimino dissipate a fortune on nonsense.'

(David Denby, *New York* magazine)

'All over Movieland, top studio bosses, major producers and show biz observers, all shell-shocked from the mindboggling 'Gate' debacle, are worrying about what it means for the industry. . . . And they are mostly blaming the power that UA gave to the arrogant Cimino. . . . Why didn't UA tell Cimino to stop? For one thing, UA had been suffering the loss of its top film execs, who left to form Orion Pictures, and was reportedly afraid to offend its remaining stars: Cimino and Woody Allen. . . .'

(Claudia Cohen, *New York Daily News*, 21 November 1980)

Going up in gunsmoke

ALAN BRIEN reports on the Cannes Film Festival

OUT of the sun at noon they come, a squadron of old-fashioned single-engined monoplanes, heading low for the uncaring beach. It is like a

criticism of a criminal, self-serving US Establishment.

The first thing that should be said about "Heaven's Gate," is that it poses as a serious, indeed

Kristofferson's renegade crat, Isobelle Huppert' woods brothel-keeper, topher Walken's alienat man.

Hollywood epic faces huge loss

From Michael Leapman
New York, Nov 21 1980

One of the most expensive films ever made seems certain to turn into Hollywood's most spectacular financial disaster. Michael Cimino's *Heaven's Gate* which cost $36m (£14.4m) to make, is being withdrawn from cinemas here only a few days after it opened, for massive surgery.

The plan is to cut the three-and-a-half hour western epic to a more manageable length and reopen it next spring. However, the reviews have been so uncompromisingly scathing that it seems unlikely that the film which stars Kris Kristof-

He signed the contract with United Artists in the wake of the success of his previous film, *The Deer Hunter*, a popular study of the Vietnam war which won him an Oscar.

When the deal was made in January, 1979, the budget for *Heaven's Gate* was set at $11.6m. It soon became clear that this was a gross underestimate. An entire town was built in Montana as the setting, 1,200 extras were hired, and Mr Cimino, a perfectionist. insisted on taking many shots dozens of times over.

It should have been finished last summer. When it was not, the release date was changed to this month but even this pro-

York Times called it " an qualified disaster " and th the *Daily News* " an al disaster".

It is about a battle bet cattlemen and settlers eastern Europe in Wyomir 1892. In the *Daily N* Kathleen Carroll wrote: " the movie been filmed ent in Russian. without English titles it might have made sense than it does in its pre state."

Vincent Canby wrote in *New York Times:* " Mr Ci has written his own screen whose awfulness has been siderably inflated by the d tor's wholly unwarranted pect for it."

No prank — that big old beech is being planted

'It must be another of those student pranks," muttered an old lady to her companion as she eyed the goings-on in Mansfield College quad.

by Chris Gray

the cranes hoisted from the trailer a 90-foot long tree trunk and planted its base firmly in the hole.

to these alterations, or that the nev look would only be short-lived.

The college, in fact, was seeing the first stage in its alteration into an American East Coast university for the shooting of scenes for a 30 millior

n defence of 'Heaven'

LIP FRENCH on Michael Cimino's latest, controversial movie.

hostility that greeted
en's Gate (Odeon, Hay-
t, X) last November has
ps more to do with the
opathology of American
an the quality of Michael
o's picture. Just as there
d some shared national
ion to will success upon
ers of the Lost Ark' this
er, so does there appear
ve been some concerted

Cimino was still reeling when
he brought his re-cut version
(reduced by an hour to 148
minutes) to Cannes, where
jackals slow-handclapped the
overture and then put a series
of insulting questions at the
subsequent press conference,
before the French critic Michel
Ciment rose to suggest that we
might talk about 'Heaven's
Gate' as a Western.

Eastern European. Only very
reluctantly do they decide to
fight, and in the process
discover some of the central
contradictions of American life.
At the film's centre are two
men, mirror-images of each
other as one of them explicitly
asserts to his own mirror-
image, both dubbed class traitors. One is the federal marshal
of Johnson County, John Av-
(Kristofferson) whom we

Heaven's Gate to be cut

"Heaven's Gate" the
40-million dollar fea-
ture film which struck
problems with Oxford
student extras during
filming in the city ear-
lier this year, is to be
drastically cut.

TS

Epic history

eter Ackroyd

aven's Gate ('X', Odeon Haymarket)

might be a good idea to set the scene.
aven's Gate was the most expensive
ematic 'flop' of recent years. It cost
ne £18 million to make, and opened in
erica to unanimous critical derision.
e director, Michael Cimino, bowed to
ssure from his studio, United Artists,
d cut the film. Now it lasts two and a half
urs rather than three and a half — there
a definite sense of its being truncated,
her as if *Henry IV* had lost an act.
Before the performance I attended, the
ema was ringed with policemen and a
monstration blocked the Haymarket.

played by K
own men, p
and the loca
Eventually t
arms agains
scenes of cc
any amount
needed. The
few men aga
against the ri
lot of violen
ter; only the

Films with
kind can al
imagination
to do anyt
confidence a
Cimino recr
transforms i
poverished i
the prairies t
frontier tow
ragged shape
American ca
migrants an

On November 4th 1980 New York's critics murdered Heaven's Gate.

Was the critics' treatment of
"Heaven's Gate" justifiable
homicide?
Now, three years on, you have
a unique opportunity to make
your own reappraisal.
From August 13-16, the
National Film Theatre is screening the original version.
In 70mm and
no less than six
times.
America,
Americans. To
put "Heaven's
Gate" in context
we've arranged a
short season of rel
ated films on the them
of immigrants (including
Kazan's rarely shown "America
America").

We think you'll find his
regard for atmosphere and
nuance a revelation.
Plus. A special screening
of "Merry Christmas, Mr.
Lawrence" as a prelude to a
major Oshima season.
Join today. A full or
associate BFI
member, can
buy tickets at
the NFT for
up to three
guests.
And you can
book in ad-
vance for only
£2.20 a ticket.
Join now
and you've got time to take your
seats for "Heaven's Gate".

On August 13th we're resurrecting it in all its glory.

Dilys's Dozen. As part of the
BFI's 50th birthday celebra-
tions, veteran critic Dilys Powell
has selected a dozen of her all-
time favourites for August.
Jacques Feyder. Our

To: Membership Dept., British Film Institute,
81 Dean Street, London W1V 6AA.

Name _____
Address _____

Please enrol me for:
☐ Full membership including free copies of
Sight & Sound. £12.25 pa.
☐ Associate membership. £7.95 pa.
I enclose a cheque/postal

Drowning in dollars

explicable success of
Hunter made its
Michael Cimino, the
darling of Hollywood
ched him, with a
t eventually climbed
d $38m, on *Heaven's
ier this year, after
ths of rumour which
er more uneasy,
Gate was unveiled in
, and then quickly
after a reception of
hostility. The
estival has just wit-
econd launching, of a
dently extensively re-
film still looks, not
matters, a lost cause,
ably excites specu-
to what part it may

million have been used up.
Paradoxically, the tragedy of
Heaven's Gate is that it has
clearly drowned in money.
From the opening sequence —
with hundreds of extras and
costumes and props decorating
an 1872 Harvard graduation that
has little or no ulterior significance in the film — the picture
is constantly slowed or halted
by huge set-pieces: vintage
railways, a roller-skating rink,
endless choreographies of extras playing immigrants, a vast,
climactic battle.

Such narrative as is identifi-
able is unceremoniously bustled
into the spaces between the set-
pieces, rather as the plot of an
old-fashioned musical takes its

to slaughter them.
Kris Kristofferson rallies the
opposition to little effect.
Isabelle Huppert, as the queen
of the local whorehouse, is
mostly undressed but occasionally puts on her clothes to
gallop pointlessly into the fray.
John Hurt and Christopher
Walken never seem clear which
side they are on, but end up
dead like everyone else apart
from Kristofferson, whose epilogue on a boat in Rhode Island,
20 years on, is as inexplicable as
the rest.
It remains to be seen whether
audiences will have the curiosity actually to pay to see this
grandiose and terrible monu-
ment to Hollywood folly, and, if

'"Heaven's Gate" – the phenomenon not the movie – has been a long time coming, but to blame it on any one director or corporate management is vastly to oversimplify what's been happening to commercial American movies over the last several decades . . . the cost of making a movie, even a modest one, has soared even faster than the cost of everything else. . . . The hits make more money than ever, while people won't go to see a flop even if it's free. . . . The pattern of the smash-hit film followed by the smash-flop film is a familiar one in today's Hollywood.'

(Vincent Canby, *The New York Times*, 30 November 1980)

AFTER THE RELEASE OF THE CUT VERSION IN APRIL 1981:
The shortened version does no better with US critics or the movie-going public and is soon withdrawn.

'Cimino has chosen the wrong story to tell . . . it's a mood piece improbably disguised as a passion play. . . . Cimino does have a real eye for epic images, and there are ravishing painterly effects . . . that are worthy of comparison with the best nineteenth-century luminist paintings, [but] Cimino aches for greatness, and his film aches from the discrepancy between his prodigious pictorialism and his primitive grasp of character and drama.'

(David Ansen, *Newsweek*)

'It is the most scandalous cinematic waste I have ever seen. . . . This is one of the ugliest films I have ever seen.'

(Roger Ebert, *Chicago Sun-Times*)

'In its two-and-a-half-hour version, Michael Cimino's *Heaven's Gate* is an experience that leaves you feeling you have witnessed a true screen epic. . . . Now it is time to sit back and enjoy all that Michael Cimino has wrought.' 'I don't think in twenty years of movie reviewing I've ever been so totally alone.'

(Kevin Thomas, *Los Angeles Times*)

AFTER THE SCREENING AT THE CANNES FILM FESTIVAL, MAY 1981: *In Europe,* Heaven's Gate *initially receives a generally critical reaction, if not expressed with the venom conveyed by American critics. In* Sight & Sound, *Penelope Houston and Richard Roud give a vivid sense of the scene at Cannes.*

'CANNES, 8.20 a.m., 20 May. At this unlikely hour, some people are actually *running* towards the Palais, bent on securing their places for the 8.30 screening of *Heaven's Gate*. Two and a half hours later, the same people no doubt join in the booing (or, more accurately, a kind of dutifully despondent mooing) which greets Michael Cimino's film. It's a curious sense of values, akin perhaps to that which makes people hang about the scenes of motorway smashes, that ensures *Heaven's Gate* the most overflowing audience of the festival's first week. And, in a sense, the audience got what they came for: in its shortened, reedited form, the film still looks like the calamity that was predicted.

'A pity, because the movie has enthusiasm and, mainly when cameraman Vilmos Zsigmond is given his head, the requisite visual flair. But it is a work of fairly spectacular irrelevances, beginning with the bravura opening of jubilation, dancing and prancing at Harvard (actually, the Sheldonian and other Oxford landmarks). The connection of this lengthy prelude with the main action, taking place twenty years later in Wyoming, is tenuous in the extreme – unless as a grotesquely roundabout and costly way of demonstrating that Marshal Kris Kristofferson's classical education comes in handy when the immigrant settlers in the Johnson County range war build Roman siege weapons. Cimino has muddled, good-hearted notions about the vices of the conniving rich in their alliance with the federal government and the virtues of the immigrant poor, though the latter's time, when not dodging bullets, seems to be spent largely on roller skates. He has an eye for an effect when he sees one. What he seemingly can't for the life of him do is hold a narrative together, tell a story that makes sense, or build a really coherent character. The price will no doubt be paid at the box office; and is paid on the screen by actors like the luckless John Hurt, whose part would seem to have been lost in the cutting room. But the real blame for the overkill should hardly be put on the director, but on a production system so enfeebled, and so easily blown away by a one-picture reputation, that it backs insecure long shots as though they were red hot favourites. The likes of Zanuck and Cohn must be laughing in their graves.'

(Penelope Houston & Richard Roud, *Sight & Sound,* **Summer 1981)**

Four months later, Philip French in the Observer *strikes a much more positive note in his thoughtful piece about the movie (still in its shortened version).*

'The hostility that greeted *Heaven's Gate* last November has perhaps more to do with the psychopathology of American life than the quality of Michael Cimino's picture. . . . In the wake of Reagan's victory, conservative critics must have been shocked by a national epic that presents a band of well-heeled xenophobic WASPs conspiring to murder hapless immigrants while the US cavalry stands idly by. Timid liberal critics were waiting to make amends to Jane Fonda for having extravagantly admired *The Deer Hunter*, a film she denounced as racist and fascist. Right and left now united in dismissing *Heaven's Gate* as incoherent, over-long, tedious.

'Their reaction reinforced . . . a feeling that the arrogant new directors needed disciplining, as Stroheim had been tamed in the 1920s, Welles in the 1940s, and Dennis Hopper in the 1960s. And who better to choose as a scapegoat than someone who had been allowed to run wildly over budget? . . .

'As a Western, *Heaven's Gate* is a handsome, intelligent, carefully considered contribution to a series of Hollywood films reappraising the frontier myth. . . . It resembles several of these fairly closely, because the same cameraman, Vilmos Zsigmond, photographed Altman's *McCabe and Mrs Miller*, the same star, Kris Kristofferson, appeared in Peckinpah's *Pat Garrett and Billy the Kid*, and the same designer, Tambi Larsen, was responsible for the appearance of Clint Eastwood's *Outlaw Josey Wales*.

'More insistently, however, than any of these, it connects the Western experience with the social crises in the burgeoning cities of the industrial north-east. Cimino presents the infamous Johnson County War of 1891, when Wyoming cattle bosses dispatched a mercenary army to punish the newly arrived homesteaders, as a microcosm of the conflict between entrenched interests and the unwelcomed huddled masses that threatened national stability and racial homogeneity. . . .

'At the film's centre are two men, mirror-images of each other, . . .both dubbed class traitors. One is the federal marshal of Johnson County, Jim Averill (Kristofferson), whom we have encountered in a prologue set in 1870 graduating from Harvard with a sense of high social duty and a belief in America as the last best hope of the world. The other is Nate Champion (Christopher Walken), a whey-faced dandy gunslinger hired by the cattlemen to execute rustlers, a man of innate decency drawn by pride and ambition to take this job. Both men share the favours of Ella Watson the local brothel-keeper who accepts cash or cattle from whoever comes to the door. Played with great warmth by Isabelle Huppert, Ella is a passionate, generous woman, at one with the land as the men are not, and representing the spirit of compromise.

'Like Visconti and Coppola, Cimino eschews carefully graded narrative in favour of powerfully animated, operatic set-pieces that are often extended beyond what puritanical northern temperaments would think reasonable limits. On the other hand, the epic, emblematic conception of character is tempered by scenes of a touching intimacy. And like *The Deer Hunter* it concludes with an ambiguous epilogue that relates personal tragedy to national experience.

'This rich bold film is not without its flaws, but they are not the yawning fissures you may have gathered from other reports.'
(Philip French, *The Observer*, 19 September 1981)

Also in September 1981, Peter Ackroyd writes an entertaining review in the Spectator. *He shares Philip French's favourable impression of the film's qualities, calling it an 'American populist epic'. But he criticizes Cimino's failure to create more than 'ciphers' as characters.*

'Before the performance I attended, the cinema was ringed with policemen . . . demonstrators turned out to be protesting against the use of animals in the film: horses were apparently wounded during violent sequences, and steers drained of their blood so that the actors' wounds would drip more realistically. Some months earlier, there were complaints from Oxford undergraduate 'extras' about Mr Cimino's treatment of people, too; they weren't drained of blood, but pretty near it. Mr Cimino can't win. . . . *Heaven's Gate* seems to be a film which . . . attracts more and more disasters until it is buried by them. This is, of course, what makes it interesting. It also happens to be a good film.

'It opens in the Harvard of 1870 on graduation day, and Mr Cimino took over Oxford University for the purpose; certainly the place has never been put to better use. If Mr Cimino has genius, it lies in the orchestration of vast numbers of people for purposes which only he can fathom – Busby Berkeley gone bananas, as hundreds of extras dance around a quad in perfect step with each other.

'But this is merely a genial foretaste of the central theme, as the plot swings forward to Wyoming, 20 years later. The story is a relatively simple one: a group of rich cattle-farmers . . . have decided to extirpate an immigrant community whom they consider to be rustlers or anarchists, or both . . . Ranged against them are the local marshal, played by Kris Kristofferson, one of their own men, played by Christopher Walken, and the local madame, Isabelle Huppert. Eventually the whole community takes up arms against [the cattle-farmers], leading to scenes of conflict and carnage for which any amount of steers' blood must have been needed. The theme is a familiar one – a few men against the 'establishment', poor against the rich, mixed with a little sex and a lot of violence. . . .

'The problem . . . is that a film which depends upon so large a tableau runs the risk of becoming unwieldy in the process. Mr Cimino's ability lies in painting with a broad brush, and his tone falters somewhat in the presentation of individuals. . . . He allows his actors to become very little more than ciphers. . . .

'But this weakness . . . can be excused in the general

extravagance and high spirits of the film: *Heaven's Gate* is an American populist epic, and we shouldn't let matters of taste stand in the way of our enjoyment of it.'
(Peter Ackroyd, *The Spectator*, 19 September 1981)

AFTER THE SALE OF UNITED ARTISTS TO MGM IN 1981:

The great American film director James Ivory is given a private screening of the movie at the old UA offices in New York, and is baffled by its harsh reception by the critics.

'Michael Cimino might be said to belong to that class of directors whose nature is to seduce and beguile by their sheer virtuosity. But even if there are some critics . . . whose nature it is like prim virgins to resist such beguilement, there must surely be others open and responsive enough . . . to be swept away by the artistry so generously displayed in *Heaven's Gate*. After all, here is a serious, progressive American film made on a grand scale with tremendous verve. Did the majority of American critics feel it was . . . a lie and a cheat and a come-on?

'I've heard indignant comment on Cimino's lack of fidelity . . . but the film expresses what a lot of people now feel might well have happened, most certainly did happen . . . in the expanding West.

'Furthermore, it seems to me that few, if any directors . . . have better expressed, given form to, the sheer dumb mass, weight, colour and brute energy of the great immigration from Europe. . . . Perhaps it was all the notoriety of his extravagant movie-making. . . . Like the reports of rich men's ostentatious feasts at the turn of the century, Cimino's efforts to "get it right" finally filled journalists and public alike with disgust so that it was decided to censure him, and his film.

'Perhaps finally it was simply a case of the audience's need for a happy ending. To have the immigrants' victory snatched at the last minute by the United States Cavalry . . . and then

to have Ella Watson shot dead as she is preparing to leave the Frontier for a better life, might have been the last straw.'
(James Ivory)

AFTER A BRIEF SHOWING ON A LOS ANGELES PAY-TV CHANNEL OF THE FULL VERSION, DECEMBER 1982: *United Artists takes the rap for having issued the cut version.*

'It seems to me a pity bordering on tragedy that the longer version was not shown [originally]. . . . Not a damned thing was gained commercially by forcing Cimino to eviscerate his work, but audiences were denied the chance to see whatever it was Cimino had in mind . . .

The moral of *Heaven's Gate* seems to be that the then-executives at United Artists poured bad judgment after bad judgment in a futile effort to make the earlier judgments look less bad.'
(Charles Champlin, *Los Angeles Times*, December 1982; the request to make the cuts had come from Cimino, but UA didn't resist the proposal)

AFTER A BRIEF SHOWING IN BRITAIN OF THE FULL VERSION IN 1983-84: *Tom Milne writes approvingly in the* Observer *that 'a major Western emerges' from the uncut version. (It is ironic that United Artists had from the outset sought to downplay the fact that it is a Western – one of the reasons for the change of title from* The Johnson County War. *Westerns as a genre had generally fallen out of fashion by the late 1970s.)*

'When Michael Cimino's *Heaven's Gate* opened in this country two years ago, shorn of 70 minutes from its running time, most critics – on the whole favourably disposed – commented on the inexplicable savagery with which the American Press tore into it.

'Now the original 219-minute version, in 70mm and with stereo sound, is briefly on view at the National Film Theatre; and bafflement over that American demolition job . . . simply escalates.

'Basically it is the same film . . . a majestic and lovingly detailed Western which simultaneously celebrates and undermines the myth of the American frontier. But that missing footage makes all the difference. . . . The opening sequence, for instance, seemed to be little more than a lavishly nostalgic, wonderfully choreographed evocation of a Harvard graduation in 1870. But the restoration of a cut speech by John Hurt shows that something else was intended. As class valedictorian, answering the ritual address by the Dean urging his graduates to spread culture through contact with the uncultivated, Hurt mockingly replies for the class that they see no need for change in a world "on the whole well arranged".

'The irony here is that as Hurt and his fellow graduate Kris Kristofferson become involved in the Johnson County Wars some 20 years later, their troubled consciences prove that the Dean was right. Watching uneasily as the rich cattle barons legally exterminate the poor immigrant farmers . . . they can only attempt to enforce the law that has become a mockery (Kristofferson) or lapse into soothing alcoholism (Hurt).

'Similarly with the strange romantic triangle that lies at the heart of the film, and which becomes much less strange when one realises that Kristofferson is already married . . . Kristofferson, sole survivor of the triangle, is seen [at the end] reunited with his wife on board a yacht, in an elegantly appointed drawing-room: strangely dreamlike settings which blandly shut out the atrocities and casuistries we have witnessed and on which the American dream was founded. A major Western emerges from this print, no question about it.'
(Tom Milne, *The Observer*, 14 August 1983)

REASSESSMENT AFTER 2012 NEW FULL-LENGTH 'DIR-
ECTOR'S CUT': *With a new full-length version overseen by Cimino
– who removed the controversial obscuring sepia tint, revealing a
much brighter, fresher print – the movie is now widely admired
and called a flawed masterpiece by many.*

'So much of *Heaven's Gate* is patently splendid that it is
mind-boggling that anyone could pronounce it an "unqualified
disaster". And the scenes which were slammed in 1980 as
being symptomatic of waste and excess – the Harvard waltz,
the massed rollerskating – are the scenes which take your
breath away.'

'The film's political concerns seem uncannily contemporary.
To see the lines of immigrants, trudging across the plains, . . . is
to be reminded of photographs of Syrian refugees. And to hear
the Stockgrowers denouncing these immigrants as "thieves
and anarchists . . ." is to imagine a screenwriter parodying
some of Donald Trump's more divisive remarks.'
(Nicholas Barber, BBC website, 4 December 2015)

'Now that the dust has settled . . . the film has steadily and
rightfully gained in appreciation.'

'If *Heaven's Gate* epitomizes the excesses of the 70s film-
brat boom in Hollywood, then it should also represent the
revolutionary spirit at its core – a determination to reject the
myths and traditions that studio filmmaking had stodgily
upheld. It's an anti-western, for starters. It's also just anti-
West, in that it's about how the civilizing forces that tamed
the country in the mid-to-late 1800s were, in fact, the villains,
violently suppressing the dreams of immigrants and other
unfortunates. Immigrants may have built America, the film
suggests, but only the few could take ownership of it.'
(Scott Tobias, *The Guardian*, 19 November 2020)

THE FILMS OF MICHAEL CIMINO

1972 *Silent Running*, Co-screenwriter (Distributor Universal Pictures)

1973 *Magnum Force*, Co-screenwriter (with John Milius), US box office $39 million (Warner Bros)

1974 *Thunderbolt and Lightfoot*, Director/Writer. US box office $21 million, production cost $4 million (United Artists)

1978 *The Deer Hunter*, Director/Co-producer/Co-writer. US box office $48 million, production cost $15 million (EMI/Universal Pictures)

1980 *Heaven's Gate,* Director/Writer. US box office $3.5 million, production and promotion cost $44 million (United Artists)

1985 *Year of the Dragon,* Director/Co-screenwriter (with Oliver Stone). US box office $18.7 million, production cost $24 million (MGM/UA Entertainment)

1987 *The Sicilian*, Director/Co-producer. US box office $5.5 million, production cost $17 million (20th Century Fox)

1990 *Desperate Hours,* Director/Co-producer. US box office $2.7 million, production cost $18 million (MGM/UA Distribution)

1996 *Sunchaser,* Director/Co-producer. US box office $30,000 (*sic*), production cost $31 million (Warner Bros)

1967 *Yesterdays* An award-winning commercial, at the start of Cimino's career in New York, made for Eastman Kodak to promote the new Kodak Instammatic camera. For a 2-minute commercial Cimino extravagantly shot 8,000 feet of film – roughly 5 hours. The shoot itself took 6 days. So highly regarded was the ad that a whole 190-page book was written about it, *The Anatomy of a Commercial: The Story of Eastman Kodak's 'Yesterdays'*.

1972 *Silent Running* Still based in New York, but with ambitions to become a movie director, Cimino engaged a Los Angeles-based agent, Michael Gruskoff, who found him work as a screenwriter on this low-budget sci-fi movie, in development for Universal Pictures. In the end the script had multiple writers, the final credit being, 'Screenplay by Deric Washburn, Michael Cimino and Steven Bochco'. The director was Douglas Trumbull, supervisor of the special effects for Kubrick's *2001: A Space Odyssey*.

1973 *Magnum Force* Realizing that to direct movies he had to be based in Hollywood, in 1971 Cimino moved to Los Angeles. His luck was in. Stan Kamen, his new and powerful agent, also represented Clint Eastwood – and Cimino was asked to write a script for the well-known spaghetti-western star. In 6 weeks he drafted *Thunderbolt and Lightfoot,* and boldly insisted he should direct it. According to Charles Elton, Cimino's biographer, Eastwood decided to take a chance on this young greenhorn, but stipulated: 'I'll give you three days. If it doesn't work, I'll get another director.'

Meantime Eastwood needed a new scriptwriter for his current project, *Magnum Force,* after John Milius dropped out. Cimino competently finished the screenplay, which was Eastwood's second outing as the San Francisco cop 'Dirty Harry'. Directed by Ted Post, the film has a climactic showdown on a deserted aircraft carrier and grossed a very respectable $39 million at the US box office for Warner Brothers.

1974 *Thunderbolt and Lightfoot* In Cimino's heist movie, Eastwood is 'The Thunderbolt', a legendary bank robber pursued by Red Leary (George Kennedy) and Eddie Goody (Geoffrey Lewis), who erroneously believe they've been double-crossed by Eastwood. Clint is rescued by Jeff Bridges as a drifter called 'Lightfoot'. Later they all team up to pull off another bank job, but Leary steals the money and beats up Lightfoot who later dies. The movie grossed $21 million at the US box office for United Artists and received generally good reviews. Nevertheless as a genre piece, perceived as an Eastwood vehicle, it didn't open any doors for Cimino in Hollywood. But effectively working for Clint, he kept his own extravagant instincts in check, and succeeded in finishing the shoot in 47 days for a completed film of 1 hour 49 minutes (109 minutes). He admired some of Eastwood's crew sufficiently to employ them again, particularly Tambi Larsen, creator of the stunning production design on *Heaven's Gate* – whose main setting, the state of Montana, had likewise been used for *Thunderbolt and Lightfoot.*

1978 *The Deer Hunter* After working fruitlessly on several screenplays, in late 1976 Cimino was hired at short notice by the British production company EMI Films, which was keen to break into the US market. They had a screenplay which they liked, but it needed adapting. Cimino agreed to rewrite the script and direct the movie. *The Man Who Came to Play* involved two soldiers in Vietnam who make money by playing rigged games of Russian roulette. Cimino, considerably aided by Deric Washburn (who later won a lawsuit to gain sole credit for the final screenplay), transformed a 'buddy movie' script into something much darker and more frightening. And they introduced a deer-hunting scene that gave its name to the final film.

We are back in 1968. Three Pennsylvania steelworkers, Mike (Robert De Niro), Nick (Christopher Walken) and Steven (John Savage) – whose wedding is a long highlight of the opening sequences – go for a last deer-hunting trip

The iconic poster for Cimino's most successful film.

before they join the airborne infantry in Vietnam. Captured by the Vietcong and kept in a cage, they are forced to play Russian roulette; Mike, however, tricks their tormentors, and they escape by clinging to a log as it is swept down a river. An army helicopter rescues them, but Steven falls into the water as they are being lifted up, breaking his legs, so Mike jumps down to save him. Nick ends up in Saigon, mentally damaged and soon a heroin addict forced to play Russian roulette for money. Through various plot twists Mike finds himself, after briefly returning to the US, back in Saigon to look for Nick (who seems to be the source of money reaching Steven in a military hospital in America). Mike tries to help Nick remember who he is as they play games of Russian roulette, but Nick aims the gun at his own head and blows his brains out. The film closes at Nick's sombre funeral in their home town where the story began. Mourners dolefully sing 'God Bless America'.

Violent and controversial, *The Deer Hunter* touched a chord among American Vietnam Vets and proved an unexpected hit with audiences – the first successful movie about an unpopular war. It was nominated for 9 Oscars and won 5 of them at the April 1979 Awards ceremony: Best Picture, Best Director, Best Supporting Actor (Christopher Walken), Best Film Editing (Peter Zinner) and Best Sound (a team of 4). Meryl Streep, playing the part of Linda, Nick's fiancée, gained her first Oscar nomination. True to his perfectionist instincts, Cimino shot 600,000 feet (about 100 hours) of film in 4 months; insisted on using 8 different US town in 4 states to represent the home town of Clairton; and chose expensive locations in Thailand (with 700 extras on a night shoot in Bangkok) for the Vietnam sequences instead of recreations on a studio back lot. The budget escalated from the contracted $7.5 million to $15 million. Although he eventually agreed to shorten his first cut of the film (3 and a half hours) by half an hour, Cimino outfoxed EMI and its US partner Universal to make that the final running time (3 hours 4 minutes; 184 minutes), rather than their preferred 160-minute version that had also been previewed. (Happily for the studios, the movie grossed $48 million at the US box office.)

Such single-minded determination and intransigence were to prove even more of a nightmare for a different studio, United Artists, on Cimino's next, even more expensive film.

1980 *Heaven's Gate* Seemingly unstoppable after his Oscars and box office success for *The Deer Hunter*, Cimino relentlessly pursued his own grand vision on *Heaven's Gate* – with little or no thought to accommodating the requests or requirements of his United Artists paymasters, or engaging positively with the media. After 9 months of shooting and printing some 1.3 million feet (220 hours) of film, and many months of editing, the result was a disastrous premiere and all that followed after that – as recounted elsewhere in this book. The movie made only $3.5 million at the US box office before being withdrawn from circulation. Some $44 million had been spent on production and promotion. Yet today it is seen as a masterpiece.

1985 *Year of the Dragon*
Inevitably, after the calamitous failure of *Heaven's Gate*, Cimino struggled to find work in Hollywood. But eventually, in early 1984, the flamboyant Italian producer Dino De Laurentiis – who drove in a Rolls Royce (as did Cimino) and could claim Jane Fonda's *Barbarella* (1968) and Milos Forman's *Ragtime* (1981) as among his film credits – offered Cimino *Year of the Dragon*. He took the view that United Artists had been to blame for not reining in the *Heaven's Gate* director. He would be different: 'forget the final cut' (ie control over the final edit) he told Cimino.

Cimino brought in Oliver Stone (Oscar-winner for the screenplay of *Midnight Express* in 1978, and later writer-director of the Vietnam movie *Platoon* (1986)) to help him rewrite the script for this story of a fight to the death between a maverick New York cop and a ganglord in Chinatown, based on a novel by Robert Daley.

Mickey Rourke was cast as Stanley White, the police captain, pitted against John Lone as Joey Tai, the Chinese Triad gang leader. White becomes romantically involved with a TV reporter, Tracy Tzu (played by Ariane), and when after various plot twists Tai rapes Tracy, the cop moves in on the ganglord at the harbour where a heroin shipment is due. Tai flees on a train bridge, leading to a showdown with both men firing recklessly at each other. Wounded in both legs, Tai commits suicide. His funeral sees White and Tracy reunited as they walk through Chinatown.

It was impossible to film in Chinatown itself, so Cimino replicated it highly effectively on a huge studio backlot in North Carolina – Stanley Kubrick even believed it to be the real thing. Running to 2 hours 14 minutes (134 minutes) and costing $24 million to make, *Year of the Dragon* grossed $18.7 million at the box office for its US distributor MGM/UA. Eventually, however, it went into profit with the addition of foreign and DVD earnings – for although the film received mixed reviews at the time and accusations of racism, it later gained a cult following. Quentin Tarantino rated the climactic train-track shoot-out as one of his favourite 'Killer Movie Moments'.

1987 *The Sicilian* De Laurentiis had made Cimino marketable again to studios as a director. In early 1986 a new company, Gladden Entertainment, offered him Mario Puzo's *The Sicilian*, a story about Michael Corleone (lead character in Puzo's *The Godfather*) and his friendship with the (real-life) Sicilian bandit Salvatore Giuliano. For legal reasons it subsequently turned out that the fictional Corleone had to be omitted, meaning the focus was now on Giuliano primarily.

Cimino cast Christopher Lambert (Tarzan in 1984's *Greystoke*) as Giuliano, whose mania for Sicilian independence in the postwar period leads him to rob from the rich and give to the poor – thereby making him popular with the people. But he becomes too big for his boots and falls out with his Mafia boss backer Don Masino Croce (a sinister Joss Ackland). Don Croce decides to have the renegade assassinated by the Don's cousin, Aspana Pisciotta (John Furturro). Terence Stamp also appears as Prince Borsa.

Although Cimino brought the shoot in on time (two-and-a-half months) and on budget ($17 million), he had to call on the help of the well-connected producers to deal with some actual Mafia trouble during the location shooting in Sicily. After 6 months of editing, he presented to his paymasters his preferred 143-minute version. This, however, exceeded the contractual maximum of 120 minutes on which he could have 'final cut'. Cimino then duly supplied the required shorter edit, but deliberately sabotaged it by omitting certain scenes that meant there were absurd jump cuts – at which the producers engaged their own editor. The resulting lawsuit between the two sides (which Cimino lost) did nothing to help publicity.

After opening in theatres on 23 October 1987, at the producers' 115-minute length, the movie made only $5.5 million for the US distributor, 20th Century Fox. Many reviewers criticized the incoherent narrative (with a poor and uncredited rewrite by Gore Vidal of a poor script), murky, amber lighting and a wooden Christopher Lambert as Giuliano. Some of the set pieces were nevertheless spectacular.

1990 *Desperate Hours* After further abortive projects, De Laurentiis again came to the rescue, offering Cimino a remake of the fine William Wyler 1955 movie *Desperate Hours*, based on the novel by Joseph Hayes and starring Humphrey Bogart. The new screenplay was by Lawrence Konner and Mark Rosenthal, and although Cimino in typical fashion cut them out of the process of writing the final script, he didn't change enough to warrant a screenplay credit after a lawsuit on the issue.

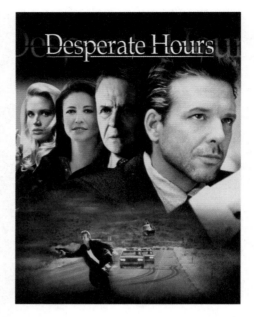

Mickey Rourke – who had also been in *Heaven's Gate* and *Year of the Dragon* – plays the sociopathic criminal Michael Bosworth, who is about to go on trial. His defence lawyer Nancy Breyers (a glamorous Kelly Lynch), inexplicably in love with Bosworth, slips him a gun so that he can escape. His brother Wally picks him up in a getaway car, and they take refuge in the home of Vietnam veteran Tim Cornell (Anthony Hopkins) and his wife Nora (Mimi Rogers), holding them hostage. Eventually the FBI surrounds the house and in a hail of bullets Bosworth and Wally are killed.

Cimino brought in the shoot 5 days ahead of schedule, on budget ($18 million), and at a reasonable 1 hour 46 minutes (106 minutes), but according to his longtime collaborator, Joann Carelli, his heart wasn't in it. Nor did he have final cut. He just needed the work. The movie opened on 5 October 1990, received generally damning reviews, and grossed only $2.7 million at the US box office for distributor MGM/UA. Yet a more recent reviewer could write that 'it bristles with drama and visual spectacle', praising its 'vivid scenes in the Colorado wilderness' (*Radio Times Guide to Films,* 2015).

1996 *Sunchaser* Cimino's final movie came to him via another maverick producer, the Israeli billionaire and Hollywood mogul Arnon Milchan, who already had such hits as *Pretty Woman* (1990) to his name. *Sunchaser* was a screenplay by Charles Leavitt for a kind of road movie mixed with spirituality and mysticism. Cimino, for whom the topic had more resonance than his other recent films, true to form ignored Leavitt, somewhat altering the script, but again not enough to earn a writer's credit after another lawsuit.

'Blue' Monroe (played by John Seda) is a 16-year-old half-Navajo member of a Los Angeles gang who has stomach cancer. He believes only a medicine man in Arizona he once met can cure him. So he kidnaps a rich and arrogant physician, Dr Michael Reynolds (a miscast Woody Harrelson), who is treating him. They drive to an Arizona reservation to visit a mountain lake sacred to the Navajo people. A New Age devotee (Anne Bancroft) tells Reynolds 'to forgive yourself for whatever has closed your heart'. A dark secret from his past is revealed as the secularist eventually begins to treat Blue as a human being and lost pilgrim.

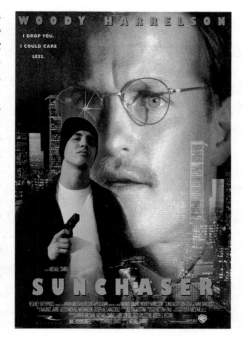

With a budget of $31 million and a running time of just over 2 hours (122 minutes), *Sunchaser* tested poorly with preview audiences. Moreover Cimino was dismissive of the producer, Milchan, which may have contributed to the decision to release the film in only a few theatres in the Southwest in September 1996, before going to DVD. It grossed a negligible $30,000 for Warner Brothers, the distributor. According to John Seda, Cimino was a troubled man during the shoot, and would frequently show up late, apparently under the influence of drugs.

FINAL WORD

Why were Cimino's last three films (*The Sicilian, Desperate Hours,* and *Sunchasers*) such commercial and in many ways artistic failures? Charles Elton, Cimino's biographer, points out that the scripts for these films were mostly the work of others. Moreover, 'He seemed unable to operate without the heady oxygen of total control – the absence of vertigo that he had felt on *The Deer Hunter* and *Heaven's Gate* – and now his sure and confident touch wavered.' (Charles Elton, *Cimino: The Deer Hunter, Heaven's Gate, and the Price of a Vision*, Abrams Press, New York 2022, p.245.) Yet the epic scale and sheer visual and emotional impact of those two remarkable movies will ensure that Cimino's reputation ultimately ranks high in the pantheon of major filmmakers.

Lithograph portraying the opening ceremony for The Great Exhibition held at Hyde Park in London. Vivian used a set of these lithographs to create his most ambitious film, *1851*, complete with soundtrack carrying extracts (edited and voiced by his wife Anne) from Queen Victoria's diary of visits to her 'beloved Albert's' showcase of the world's arts and industries.

PART III

VIVIAN RIDLER: MOVIE BUFF AND ACCOMPLISHED AMATEUR FILMMAKER

GENESIS OF A PASSION AND KEY FILMS

Vivian Ridler's enthusiasm for film, as manifested in his *Diary of an Extra*, didn't come from nowhere. Far from it, as the following brief account explains.

Born in 1913, he grew up during the early years of cinema – an art form of great appeal to someone with his strong visual bent. Although he would make his career as a typographer and printer (eventually running the printing division of Oxford University Press for 20 years, from 1958 to 1978), film and photography were always very close to his heart. He delighted in telling his four children (Jane, Kate, Ben and Colin – the first two of whom we have met in the Diary) how in Bristol during his youth he had been taught piano by a lady who played music to accompany silent movies. Those same children were entertained at home with film screenings showing Charlie Chaplin and Buster Keaton, just as these stars had once held Vivian spellbound. Transfixed he had been too by the technical wizardry of Abel Ganz's 1927 silent epic *Napoléon*.

By the time Vivian was in his late teens the Talkies had come in; he wrote this in another diary some 40 years later:

'To London on 12.30 train . . . Saw Lubitsch's *The Love Parade* (1930) at the Nat. Film Theatre. Stood up very well, tho' Chevalier ghastly. *Lupino Lane* excellent. I first saw it in 1931 at the giant Regal in Bristol.'

The next day he writes, on 'another visit to the N F Theatre . . .
> I saw *42nd Street*, made in 1933. I remember seeing it in Bristol
> at the time and apart from the outstanding absence of talent
> in Ruby Keeler, the principal, it was enjoyable.'
> (*Diary of a Master Printer*, The Perpetua Press 2022, p.98)

Similarly, in yet another diary he kept during 1943, when he was
serving as a radio signalman with the RAF in Nigeria, he records
going to see in his time off some 50 or more films. He assesses
them with a critical eye (and ear), for example on 23 June: 'Saw
Top Hat again, after about 8 years. It didn't wear well, although
the songs by Irving Berlin still sounded good.' Or on 9 July:
'Saw *Flame of New Orleans*, an American film made by René Clair
. . . I noticed again how much of the particular Clair atmosphere
is provided by the music. Only Preston Sturges seems to have
attempted to help comedy in this way: his early films copy Clair
closely, particularly in the rushing of people along corridors &
up stairs etc.'

Nevertheless until the postwar years it was still photography
rather than filmmaking that Vivian practised himself. He took
fine portraits of his wife, the poet Anne Ridler, and of his young
children, the first of whom – Jane – was born in 1941. Then, during
a holiday with Anne in Venice in the early 1950s, his precious
high-quality still camera was stolen. This seems to have spurred
a change to cinematography. As usual in his life, he set about the
process with meticulous preparation. In one corner of his study in
the family home at 14 Stanley Road in Oxford he built himself a
neat editing desk. Here he would sit for hours, spooling the 8mm
film from a 'short' he had shot to and fro through the small monitor
fixed to the rear of the desk. This allowed him to assess where to cut
a scene and splice it back onto the adjacent section of film, so as to
create a smoothly flowing narrative that had pace but not jerkiness.

From his earliest years Vivian had loved to draw. And as an avid
reader of magazines such as *American Cinematographer, Sight*

and Sound, and *Films and Filming* he soon learned the value of sketching a storyboard in order to map out visually the narrative for the more elaborate films he came to make. As for the actual filmmaking equipment, he tended to use a Bolex ciné-camera coupled with Kodachrome I colour film stock – he liked its warm tones – subsequently moving on to Kodachrome II.

What of the films themselves? From the mid-1950s to the mid-1980s he produced a great array of comedies, adventure and ghost stories, documentaries, art films, family diaries and quite elaborate records of travel abroad. The first substantial comedy, *Tip & Run* (1957), has Ben and Colin tip Kate out of a deck chair where she is happily dozing, the ensuing pursuit round the house allowing Vivian to try shooting a classic movie 'chase sequence'. *Slipped Disc* (1964) shows Vivian, alone in the house while his wife is at church, putting on Colin's Shadows record to have a go at doing the Twist – then in vogue – ricking his back in the process. What to do? He hobbles into the garden so as to pretend his crippled state comes from virtuously digging the vegetable patch. And *The Thirteenth Candle* (1965), filmed partly at Colin's birthday party, has a friend substitute a firework for one of the candles, the resulting explosion blasting a boy on to the top of the kitchen cupboard – for which the film director is able to try out various special effects.

Two shorts pay tribute to Hollywood in their film titles: *The Boys Who Ate Too Much* (1957) echoes Hitchcock's 1956 remake, starring James Stewart and Doris Day, of his 1934 thriller *The Man Who Knew Too Much*; while *Bad Day at Big Rock* (1959), featuring a French boy (on an exchange with Ben) as a villain, calls to mind the John Sturges 1955 neo-Western *Bad Day at Black Rock*, starring Spencer Tracey.

Vivian himself made quite a long 'thriller' (called the Epic by the family) in 1958-59: *The Fortune Hunters* features Colin, a boy on a quest, fishing a bottle from the lake at Blenheim that contains a colourful map of the Cornish peninsula (drawn by the director) and the words 'Here Be Treasure' with an arrow pointing to a headland at St Mawes. Unfortunately for our hero a robber, played by Ben, has been watching and sets off in pursuit. Vivian had great fun filming pre-Beeching-cuts trains, in their handsome dark red and cream livery, as the boys travel to Cornwall. The climax shows Colin – sack of treasure over his shoulder – being confronted by Ben on the headland and using the sack to knock his foe into the sea below. (The question of whether or not the robber is meant to have drowned became a bone of contention between the boys' parents!)

Colin gets his comeuppance in *Nought for Behaviour* (1961), where his real-life delinquent behaviour of smoking secretly with his chum Bobby in the shed at the bottom of the garden is portrayed as a story with a moral, the climax here – after they're discovered – being that Colin feels sick at the very sight of food. The film's title is probably a play on the remarkable *Zéro de Conduite* (1933) by Jean Vigo, about rebellious schoolchildren.

The Beeching cuts to the rail network had taken effect by the time Vivian came to make one of his simplest but most evocative short films in 1964, *The End of the Line*. By now he had at his disposal a synchronized soundtrack (for this film a clever use of uncopyrighted doleful mood music). He employed an ingenious British machine called the Cinecorder, specifically designed so that magnetic tape – on to which the soundtrack was recorded – could be linked to, and control the speed of, a film projector during a screening. In 1963 Vivian made a powerful ghost story, *A Voice from the Past*, that had a complicated soundtrack combining music (Stravinsky's *Rite of Spring* played at 16rpm!) with a narrator's voiceover. The plot was derived by Anne partly from Kipling's 1890 short story, 'The End of the Passage'. The setting is the mysterious Monkhaven, below St Ishmael's in Pembrokeshire, so-named because of its use in early medieval times by Christians seeking safety from marauders. Curious stone battlements in the bay and on the cliff above, follies dating from the time of the Crimean War, add to the oddness of the place. In the film a tall schoolfriend of Ben's plays the part of a hooded monk's ghost, which frightens Colin and another boy. They duly discover that the monk has been wrongfully buried in unconsecrated ground, and their detective work means his tortured soul can now be released to rest in peace.

Another film with a religious theme, *The Tenant in the Tower* (1965) – Vivian's longest at half an hour – is set in the University Church of St Mary's in Oxford. Andy Vernède, the elder brother of Colin's friend Nicky Vernède (who had himself co-starred in the Monkhaven film), plays the part of a fugitive holed up in the church tower, whom the Sunday School children encounter.

As well as many family and holiday diaries, Vivian shot a large number of documentaries – valuable records often of activities in and around Oxford, such as *St Giles Fair* (1959), the building of *Donnington Bridge* (1960-62), and *House Extension* (1962), the last covering the construction of a new part of the house at 14 Stanley Road (Vivian showed the completed film later to the workmen, one of whom remarked of himself, 'I look just like a little ol' turtle'). *A Dragon's Life* (1960-61), featured Colin in his early years at the school, with some of the masters, 'Clarkey', 'Inky' and Dougie Dalrymple among them.

Before natural history programmes became ubiquitous on television, Vivian's *The Flycatchers* (1969) was unusual and proved a big hit with friends in Oxford given a filmshow. It arose through serendipity. In the 1960s and 1970s the family regularly holidayed at High Bield, a cottage in Little Langdale Valley in the Lake District that belonged to the painter Delmar Banner (whose portrait of Beatrix Potter hangs in the National Portrait Gallery) and his wife, the sculptor Josefina de Vasconcellos (whose fine work can be found in several British cathedrals). In 1969, there nesting in the arch of the cottage front porch were two flycatchers with a very young brood. Vivian, dedicated to his art, gave up much of his fortnight's holiday to patiently filming this nest (with nothing more than a handheld camera) as the fledglings grew larger and larger, and the parents more and more frantic in their efforts to feed the offspring. Would the holiday end before the young birds took wing? It was touch and go. Coupled with wide-angle views of the valley, with its picturesque stone bridge and mountain crags in the background, as well as a soundtrack allowing us to hear the flycatchers calling to each other, this is one of Vivian's most successful short films.

His cinematic imagination could be fired not just by bird life but by still life too. He had the clever idea of using close-ups to look in detail at two pictures he had at home: *Adam and Eve* (1964), an 18th-century engraving of the Garden of Eden, after Jan Brueghel the Younger (1601-1678); and *The Boat Race* (1964), a 19th-century colour lithograph showing steamships following the Oxford and Cambridge rowers on the Thames. The Brueghel, far too dense to take in from a distance, comes alive as the camera scans across all the creatures depicted. For *The Boat Race*, the voice of John Snagg on the soundtrack gives a sense of drama and momentum as he describes in a radio broadcast the progress of a much later such event. Victorian figures, perched in trees to get a better view of the action (and heard cheering on the soundtrack) wouldn't normally catch the eye.

The culmination of this close-up technique came with *1851* (1966), possibly the most important film Vivian made. In a vivid and extraordinary way, it recreated for the viewer the sense of actually being present at the Great Exhibition, Prince Albert's triumphant show displaying manufactures from round the world that was held in the Crystal Palace at Hyde Park. How was this recreation possible? The innovative decision had been made at the time to record, through large-scale colour lithographic prints, a great number of halls at the exhibition. One set of these prints had come into the possession of John Johnson (a predecessor of Vivian's as University Printer), whose considerable collection of printed ephemera was held at Oxford University Press. Before the whole collection was transferred by Vivian to the Bodleian Library, he borrowed some of the lithographs, taking them home and mounting each one in turn – following the storyboard sequence he had drawn out – on a special wooden frame he had constructed.

Using a Meccano motor to raise the prints up and down, and with a horizontal slide in front for his Bolex ciné-camera, he could film vertical, horizontal and diagonal shots of details in the lithographs. Anne meantime had put together a script based on Queen Victoria's diaries describing visits to her 'beloved Albert's' exhibition. The soundtrack consisted of Anne impersonating Victoria, interspersed with bursts of Rule Britannia and culminating in Handel's Hallelujah Chorus sung at the closing ceremony. It made a rousing and riveting film which Philip Larkin, when shown it at a dinner party held in his honour at Stanley Road in 1970, rightly called 'a work of art'.

The Films of Vivian Ridler: A Chronological List

S=Soundtrack
Numerals indicate numbered labels on VR's film reels

1956
Cranmer 1. Moments from performance in University Church of St Mary's, Oxford of Anne Ridler's verse play, *The Trial of Thomas Cranmer,* commissioned to commemorate the 400th anniversary of the actual trial held in the church
On the Rocks 115. Family comedy filmed in Cornwall featuring District Nurse Audrey Wheeler
The Boys Who Ate Too Much 101. Comedy: Colin and a friend gorge on ice cream
Hudnall 101. Last home of Violet Bradby, Anne Ridler's mother
Christmas 103, 172
Family Diary 171

1957
Tip & Run 115. First substantial comedy, with Kate, Ben & Colin
Magic Charlie 115. Anne mesmerises Colin by making a card cutout of Charlie Chaplin dance when suspended on a line
Colin's Birthday 103
Port Holland 102. Holiday with Audrey Wheeler
Lyme Regis 107
Seatown 173
Swiss Holiday 108
Lake Leman; Lausanne Fair 106

Roland Rhythm 105. Printing machine in action

1958
The Fortune Hunters S 165. 'Thriller' as Colin seeks his fortune, pursued by Ben as a robber
Horse Show; River Scenes 174
Family Diary 109
Timson Rotary 110. Another printing machine in action

1959
St Giles Fair S 112
Bad Day at Big Rock 104. Story filmed on the Pembrokeshire coast with Ben's French exchange Aymar, who fires at Ridler family members with a catapult and dives from a high rock to evade capture
Corn on the Cobb 104. Consuming candyfloss on the sea front at Lyme Regis
Backwater 104. Low tide documentary
Cardigan; Coracle Races 111. Record of the ancient tradition of paddling coracles in a river
Verona 111
Jane Teaching at the Crescent School 147
Colin's Birthday Party 172
Walk in the Sun 152
Old Moore's Almanack 172
Urania Printing Machine 3
Family Diary 176

1960
France 168. Holiday record
Holland 177
New York 169 Business trip
Niagara Falls 114
Christmas 173

1960-61
A Dragon's Life 166,167. Record of part of Colin's time at the prep school, featuring some of the masters and lessons; includes notorious 'clothes test' in the river that a boy had to pass to prove he could swim; filmed largely in black & white

1960-62
Donnington Bridge 124. Documentary in black & white of the construction of the new road bridge across the Thames, and removal of the old footbridge

1961
Nought for Behaviour S 180. Morality tale: Colin and his friend Bobby secretly take up smoking in their shed at the bottom of the garden; but it makes Colin want to vomit at the sight of food, and Anne finds cigarettes as she empties out his pockets when he retires to bed; filmed in black & white
After the Ball S 179. Brief story featuring a large yellow ball on a Cornish beach

Portscatho; Low Tide 152
Family Diary 178

1962
Saw Point 181
Pembroke 181
Fishing at Lyme 181
*On the Brink; Aisholt;
Blenheim* 117
Brunel & Bristol 123
House Extension 114.
Record of the construction
of the sitting-room
extension at 14 Stanley
Road, Oxford, by Hinkins
& Frewin, the builders
Fruitful Meeting S 182.
On a family holiday at
Aisholt in Somerset Colin
& his friend Nicky
Vernède are recorded
obsessively feeding a
horse with vast numbers
of fallen apples
Christmas Present S 182
Family Diary 116

1963
A Voice from the Past S
161. Ambitious ghost story
shot in colour at
Monkhaven, below St
Ishmael's in
Pembrokeshire, featuring
Colin & Nicky Vernède
who encounter the ghost
of a monk, played by Ben's
Clifton schoolfriend
Douglas Allford. The voice
of a narrator and
Stravinsky's *Rite of
Spring* (at half-speed!)
form the soundtrack.
Cakes & Pains S 118.
Comedy
Austria S 119. Holiday
documentary
St Ishmael's Fair 120
*The Sea Shall Not Have
Them* 120. Comedy

Family Diary 122
Oxford Scenes 113

1964
Adam and Eve S 6. Film in
close-up of this
18th-century engraving,
after Brueghel the
Younger, of the Garden of
Eden; Agfa Gevaert film
using Chinon ciné-camera
The Boat Race S 121.
Another documentary
using close-ups, of a
19th-century colour
lithograph showing the
Oxford and Cambridge
boat race; the noise of
crowds cheering and the
voice of the broadcaster
John Snagg form the
soundtrack
The End of the Line S 121.
Highly evocative short
documentary, comprising
almost entirely shots from
above moving along an
empty railway track to the
accompaniment of
melancholy mood music
Slipped Disc S 180.
Comedy: not taking
himself too seriously,
Vivian is filmed
surreptitiously trying to
do the Twist to the sound
of Shadows music, ricking
his back, and then
staggering into the garden
in order to pretend to his
wife that he has injured
himself digging in the
vegetable patch
Farnborough Airshow S
186. Documentary with
Vulcan, Victor, VC10 and
Bristol aircraft
Near Miss S 183. Family
story filmed in
Pembrokeshire

*Wales: Pembrokeshire,
Gower Peninsula,
Brecon* 185
Family Diary (printing
Christmas card etc) 184
Bible Production 164.
Documenting the printing
of the *New English Bible*
at Oxford University
Press (OUP)
Jordan Hill 4.
Documentary at OUP's
North Oxford warehouse

1965
The 13th Candle S 187
Comedy set at Colin's
birthday party, where
Nicky Vernède has
replaced one candle with a
firework which explodes,
propelling a boy on to the
top of a cupboard and
causing mayhem;
Ferrania filmstock
The Tenant in the Tower
S 162. Vivian's longest
feature film, set in the
University Church of St
Mary the Virgin in
Oxford, with Andy
Vernède playing a fugitive
hiding in the church
tower, where Sunday
School children encounter
him; Agfa Gevaert film
using Bolex & Chinon
ciné-cameras
Tulips in Holland 193;
Kodachrome II using
Chinon ciné-camera
High Bield 189. The first of
many holidays in this
Lake District cottage in
Little Langdale Valley
belonging to Delmar
Banner and his wife
Josefina de Vasconcellos,
he a painter, she a
sculptor; Kodachrome II

using Chinon

Moss Rigg 10.
Documentary of this
atmospheric slate quarry
on the side of Wetherlam
above Little Langdale
Valley; Kodachrome II,
Chinon

Karin (1) 190. Jane's
daughter Karin as an
infant; Agfa Gevaert film,
Chinon

Snell Family Robinson 8

Family Diary 188

**Up the Creek with St
John Ambulance** 8.
Recording a trip with this
group attached to OUP

1966

**1851: The Great
Exhibition** S 196.
Elaborate documentary
using close-ups of
lithographs showing the
different exhibits, with a
script written and
narrated by Anne based
on Queen Victoria's
diaries, accompanied by
music by Handel; Vivian
drew a frame-by-frame
storyboard and had a
wooden stand constructed
to support the lithographs
as he filmed each one;
shot in Agfacolor CK17

France 192. Holiday
documentary;
Kodachrome II

Pont du Gard S 194.
Record of this famous
Roman viaduct;
Kodachrome II

The Lakes S 163;
Kodachrome II, Bolex
ciné-camera

Queer Quarry 193. Story
set in Lake District;
Kodachrome II, Bolex

Strictly for the Birds 12

Amahl 11. Menotti opera
*Amahl & the Night
Visitors* in which Ben sang
one of the three kings,
performed at the
University Church of St
Mary's; Ferrania film,
Bolex

Karin (2) 191; Agfa Gevaert
film

Diary 195

1967

**The Lakes: High Bield;
the Birds at St Bee's**
125; 133; Kodachrome II,
Bolex

Ireland 128. Holiday
documentary;
Kodachrome II, Bolex

New York 170.
Documentary of a
business visit showing
Empire State Building
and liner *United States*;
Agfacolor, Bolex

**Karin & Juliette as
infants** 52, 53, 126-127,
Agfacolor, Bolex

Down the Strand 26

1968

Kate's Wedding 13.
Kodachrome II, Bell
Howell ciné-camera

South Germany S 129
Holiday documentary with
Rolf's home town of
Münsingen, Jane, Karin
& Juliette; Kodachrome
II; Bolex

Luxembourg 130

Colin as 'Hamlet' 17,
Acting the part at
Magdalen College School
aged 16; Perutz 400 ASA
black & white film, Bell
Howell

Azalea; Magdalen Water

Walk 14

OUP Extension 28-30, 44,
Record of the construction
of the 100,000 sq ft
extension to the printing
works

Cambridge 136, 160

1969

The Flycatchers S 133
Nature film as two adult
birds, nesting in the porch
at High Bield, frantically
feed their ever-growing
offspring, dashing to the
small lake in the valley
below to catch insects,
chirruping to each other
as they do so; Kodachrome
II, Bolex hand-held

The Magic Man S 132
Story for Karin & Juliette
featuring a wind-up
plastic figure;
Kodachrome II, Bolex

Spain S 155
Holiday documentary
(following a printers'
conference in Madrid), in
which Vivian, Anne & Ben
visit Salamanca, Segovia,
Ávila, Toledo and the
strange region of Las
Hurdes (filmed in 1933 by
Luis Buñuel);
Kodachrome II, Bolex

1970

Greece I & II S 156, 157
Holiday documentary of a
circular tour by car of
ancient sites, from Athens
north to Delphi then south
to Olympia and round to
Mycenae, Epidaurus,
Mystra and back to
Athens; Kodachrome II,
Bolex

The Lakes 135
Kodachrome II, Bolex

On a Summer Afternoon
144
The Snells; Karin &
Juliette

1971
Sicily 158,159
Holiday documentary of
a round trip by car, from
Syracuse along the south
coast to Agrigento and
Selinunte, and north via
Segesta to medieval
Monreale and Palermo,
finally diagonally back via
Roman villa of Piazza
Armerina to Catania;
Kodachrome II, Bolex

1972
Augop, Radnorshire 138
The Lakes 137

1973
Yorkshire 153. First visit to
Beverley & Westwood
View, Castle Howard etc;
Bolex
France (Loire) 134.
Kodachrome II
Cambridge 160

1974
Tiny Troubles S 145.
Children's story
The Lakes 137

1975
Ramsay Island 19
*Lindisfarne; Colin's
String Quartet* 20

1976
Porlock 22. Somerset
village where Ridler
ancestors are buried
Rome 139. Holiday
documentary;
Kodachrome II
Yorkshire 141. Sledmere
etc; Dan as infant;
Kodachrome II

1977
Africa 140. Business trip to
Nigeria & Kenya
North Wales 45-47. Dan's
first steps; Lleyn
Peninsula; Kodachrome II

1978
Toby as infant 142,
Kodachrome II
Augop 142

1979
Turkey 146. Holiday
documentary: Istanbul
(with military crackdown),
then Kusadasi, Ephesus,
Heracleia, Didyma &
Miletus
Beverley 142
Dan & Toby 143

1980
Heaven's Gate 50. Vivian's
role as an extra during
filming in Oxford on this
Mike Cimino movie (very
brief shots)
Meadow Mischief 49. A
tale set on Port Meadow,
where Karin, Juliette &
friends go pony-riding and
an accident precipitates a
chase
On Skomer; Broadhaven
51

1981
On Derwentwater 54

1982
Snowbound 151

1982-1983
Family Faces

1984
Pembrokeshire 56. Holiday
with the Wilsons

1985
Young Sherlock Holmes
57. The Wilson boys

Further Reading

Titles marked with an asterisk (*) are of particular relevance to *Heaven's Gate* and Cimino

*Bach, Steven *Final Cut: Art, Money and Ego in the Making of Heaven's Gate*, Rev Edn (Newmarket Press, New York 1991)
  The classic, bestselling and highly partial account of the making and unmaking of the movie, written by the key figure at United Artists who had to deal with Cimino during and after the shoot.

*Biskind, Peter *Easy Riders, Raging Bulls: How the Sex, Drugs, and Rock 'n' Roll Generation Saved Hollywood* (Simon & Schuster, New York 1998)
  Just as *Final Cut* is a brilliant page-turner dissecting the *Heaven's Gate* debacle, so *Easy Riders, Raging Bulls* takes a broader look at the rise and fall of the Hollywood auteur-director during the 1970s in a pacily written and well-informed narrative.

Bliss, Michael *Martin Scorcese and Michael Cimino* (Scarecrow Press, Metuchen, NJ 1985)

*Cimino, Michael *Conversations en miroir* (Gallimard, Paris 2004)
— *Big Jane (a novel)* (Gallimard, Paris 2001)

*Elton, Charles *Cimino: The Deer Hunter, Heaven's Gate, and the Price of a Vision* (Abrams Press, New York 2022)
  The first full-length biography of the director, a readable and skilfully constructed account of Cimino's whole career as well as his mysterious persona.

Heard, Christopher *Mickey Rourke: High and Low* (Plexus, London 2006)

*Hickenlooper, George *Reel Conversations: Candid Interviews with Film's Foremost Directors and Critics* (Citadel Press, New York 1991)
  Includes a rare and extensive interview with Cimino, a decade after *Heaven's Gate*.

Kezich, Tullio and Alessandra Levantesi *Dino: The Life and Films of Dino De Laurentiis* (Hyperion, New York 2004)

Levy, Shawn *De Niro: A Life* (Crown, New York 2014)

McGilligan, Patrick *Clint: The Life and Legend* (St Martin's Press, New York 2002)

Ridler, Vivian *Diary of a Master Printer,* Edited by Colin Ridler (Perpetua Press, Oxford 2022)
  Focuses on a crucial year during his time as Printer to the University, Oxford, and the films of his own he was showing to friends as well as classic films he was watching again at the BFI after first seeing them in the 1930s.

Schickel, Richard *Clint Eastwood: A Biography* (Knopf, New York 1996)

Thomson, David *The New Biographical Dictionary of Film,* Sixth Edition (Little Brown, London 2014; Knopf, New York 2014)
— *The Whole Equation: A History of Hollywood* (Knopf, New York 2004; Vintage, London 2006)

*Thoret, Jean-Baptiste *Michael Cimino: Les voix perdues de l'Amerique* (Flammarion, Paris 2013)

Sources of Illustrations

Illustration credits by page number, a=above, b=below

1 Ridler Archive
2 © United Artists
8 Ridler Archive
10 Ridler Archive
13 Ridler Archive
20 Ridler Archive
21 Ridler Archive
23a Courtesy of the BFI National Archive
23b Ridler Archive
27 Ridler Archive
30 Ridler Archive
31 Ridler Archive
36–37 Ridler Archive
38–39 Photo 12/Alamy Stock Photo
41 © United Artists
44 Photo by John Minihan/Hulton Archive/Getty Images
46 © United Artists
48 Ron Galella/Getty Images
51 Ronald Grant Archive/Mary Evans
54 © EMI
57 Courtesy of the BFI National Archive
58 United Archives Gmbh/Alamy Stock Photo
59 Allstar Picture Library Limited/Alamy Stock Photo
61 Entertainment Pictures/Alamy Stock Photo
62–63 Maximum Film/Alamy Stock Photo
65 Everett Collection Inc./Alamy Stock Photo
66 © United Artists
67 © United Artists
70 Courtesy of the BFI National Archive
77 Ron Galella/Getty Images
79 Everett Collection Inc./Alamy Stock Photo
84 Ridler Archive
90–91 Ridler Archive
104 © EMI
106 © MGM
107 © Twentieth Century Fox Film Corporation
108 © MGM
109 © Warner Brothers
110 Royal Collection Trust

Index

Page numbers in *italic* refer to the illustrations

ABC, Oxford 42
Academy Awards 69, 85, 87
Ackland, Joss 107
Ackroyd, Peter 96–98
The African Queen 52
Albeck, Andy 53, 68, 69, 71–72, 74
Albert, Prince Consort 110, 117–18
Alden's, Oxford 12, 27
Alden's Field, Oxford 15, 17
Allan, Alkan 40n
Allen, Woody 53, 82, 89
Altman, Robert 82, 95
Ansen, David 92
Apocalypse Now 52, 74, 78
Averill, James 55, 57–64

Bach, Steven 53, 68–69, 71–72, 74
Final Cut 53, 69
BAFTA 7, 87
Bancroft, Anne 109
Bangkok 50, 105
Banner, Delmar 116
Barber, Nicholas 101
Bart, Peter 78
BBC 7, 40n, 101
Benjamin, Robert 52–54, 68
Berkeley, Busby 97
Berlin, Irving 113
Birth of a Nation 51
Biskind, Peter, *Easy Riders, Raging Bulls* 49, 53
Blake, Lord (Robert) 29 and n
Bochco, Steven 102
Bodleian Library, Oxford 29, *30*, 117
Bogart, Humphrey 52, 108
Bogdanovich, Peter 48
Bolex 114, 118
Bond, James 14, 52

Bonnie and Clyde 51
Boorman, John 82
The Borgias (BBC series) 40n
Bridges, Jeff 59, *62*, 74, *77*, 87, 103
Bridges, John 59, 64
Bristol 112, 113
Brueghel, Jan the Younger 117
Butch Cassidy and the Sundance Kid 54
Butler, Janet 17–18
Butler, Ted 17–18

Canby, Vincent 88, 92
Cannes Film Festival 78, 81, 93
Canton, Frank 55, 59, 64
Carelli, Joann 47–48, *48*, 68, 69, 72, 79, 108
Casper, Wyoming 58, *58*, 60, 71
Catte Street, Oxford 26, 28, *30*, 32, *44*, 75
Chabrol, Claude 86
Champion, Nate 55, 58, 60, 64
Champlin, Charles 99
Chaplin, Charlie 52, 112
Chicago Sun-Times 92
Cimino, Michael 11, *20–21*, *27*, *44*, *48*, *77*
  as a screenwriter 49–50
  budget for prologue 75
  budget overspend 25n, 53, 69–74, 105
  chronology of *Heaven's Gate* 67–79
  death 79
  'Director's Cut' of *Heaven's Gate* 78–79, *79*, 101
  early life 47–49
  The Deer Hunter 6, 19, *48*, 50–54, *51*, *54*, 68, 69, 82, 85, 88, 89, 95, 96, 103,

  104, 105
  fee for *Heaven's Gate* 69
  filming in Oxford 6–7, 19, 25–26, 29–31, 34, 40, 75
  films 102–109
  first screening of *Heaven's Gate* 75
  on *Heaven's Gate* 80–82
  reputation as a difficult director 52
  reviews of *Heaven's Gate* 51, 88–101, *90–91*
  script for *Heaven's Gate* 53–55, 67
  shortened version of *Heaven's Gate* 76, 92–94, 99
  VR sees film 42, 43
Cinecorder 115
Clair, René 113
Clarendon Building, Oxford 28
Classic cinema, Shaftesbury Avenue, London 42–43
Close Encounters of the Third Kind 50, 82
Cohen, Claudia 89
Cook, Brian *20*
Cooper, Gary 52, 72
Coppola, Francis Ford 48, 49, 52, 69, 74, 78, 96
Cornwell, Peter 24
Cotten, Joseph 19, 22–26, *23*, 57
Crabtree, John 14–15, 16–17

Daily Variety 73
Daley, Robert 106
Dalrymple, Dougie 116
Day, Doris 114
De Laurentiis, Dino 106, 107, 108
De Niro, Robert 50, 103
De Palma, Brian 82
The Deer Hunter 6, 19, *48*, 50–54, *51*, *54*, 68, 69, 82,

85, 88, 89, 95, 96, 102, 103, *104,*105
Denby, David 89
Desperate Hours 102, 108, *108*, 109
Doctor Zhivago 53
Durante, Jimmy 24 and n

Eastwood, Clint 49, *67*, 73, 95, 103
Ebert, Roger 92
Elton, Charles 47, 49, 103, 109
EMI Films 49–50, 72, 105
Equity 11, 26
Ethiopia 14, 16–17

FAA 34
Fairbanks, Douglas 52
Fazan, Eleanor 33n, 75
Field, David 53, 68–69, 71–74
Films in Review 88
Fonda, Jane 95, 106
Ford, John 48, 64, 65
Forman, Milos 106
French, Philip 95–96
Furturro, John 107

Ganz, Abel 112
Gapay, Lee 73
Glacier National Park 69–71
Gladden Entertainment 107
Godard, Jean-Luc 86
The Godfather 78
Golden Globes 83, 86, 87
Granada TV 32
Great Exhibition, London (1851) *110*, 117
Griffith, D W 52
Gruskoff, Michael 102
The Guardian 101

Haile Selassie, Emperor of Ethiopia 16
Harrelson, Woody 109
Harrison, Benjamin 55
Harvard Chapel 19, 22, 24
Harvard University 6, 11, 12, 43, 57, 94, 96, 97, 100,

101
Harvey, Jim 69
Hawkes, Howard 48
Hayes, Joseph 108
Heaven's Gate 57–59, 61–63, 65, 70
  auditions for extras *10*, 11–12
  budget overspend 15 and n, 25n, 50, 53, 68–74, 83, 89, 105
  call sheets *13*
  chronology 67–79
  Cimino on 80–82
  costumes 12–17, 40, 71, 75
  credits 56
  'Director's Cut' 78–79, *79*, 101
  filming in Oxford 6–7, 17–27, *23*, 28–40, *30–31*, *36–39*, 75
  first screening 75
  Kristofferson on 83–85
  length 74, 75
  plot 57–64
  posters *Frontispiece, 41*, *46, 66*
  premieres 40, 76, 77
  reviews 42, 49, 51, 76, 88–101, *90–91*
  script 53–55, 67
  shortened version 76, 78, 92–94, 99
  takings 76
  VR sees 42–43
Hertford College, Oxford 28
Hickenlooper, George 80–81
High Noon 52, 68
Hitchcock, Alfred 114
Homestead Act (1862) 54–55
Hopkins, Anthony 108
Hopper, Dennis 95
House of Commons 17
Houston, Penelope 93–94
Howe, Geoffrey 17
Huppert, Isabelle *Frontispiece*, 40n, 42, *46*, 59, *62*, 69, 72, 76, *77*, 86, 96, 97
Hurt, John 57, 86–87, 94

filming in Oxford 19, *20*, 22–26, *23*, 28–31, 32, 34, *44, 57*
in Montana 73
reviews 100
VR sees film 42, 43

In the Heat of the Night 52
Irvine, Billy 55, 57, 59, 64, 65
Isis 84, *84*
Ivory, James 98–99

Johnson, John 117
Johnson County War (1891) 53–55, 58–60, 94, 95–96, 100
The Johnson County War 52, 53, 67, 68–69, 99
  see also Heaven's Gate

Kalispell, Montana 69–71, 72
Kamen, Stan 49, 68, 103
Katz, Lee 69
Kavanagh, Derek 71
Keaton, Buster 112
Keeler, Ruby 113
Kennedy, George 103
Kennedy, John 81
Kent, Nicolas 6–7, *84*
Kerkorian, Kirk 76
King Kong 51
Kipling, Rudyard 115
Kodachrome 114
Kodak 102
Konner, Lawrence 108
Krim, Arthur 52–54, 68
Kristofferson, Kris 11, 19, *20*, 25, 26, 57, 71, 72, 87, 94
  fee 69
  filming in Oxford 6–7, 28, 29, 31, *44, 57*, 75, 32
  on *Heaven's Gate* 79
  posters *Frontispiece, 46*
  VR sees film 42, 43
  reviews 95, 96, 97, 100
Kubrick, Stanley 81, 102, 106

Ladd, Alan 54
Lambert, Christopher 107
Länge, Jane (VR's daughter) 29 and n, 112, 113
Larkin, Philip 118
Larsen, Tambi 95, 103
Last Tango in Paris 52
Lawrence of Arabia 53
Lean, David 72
Leavitt, Charles 108
Lewis, Geoffrey 103
Little Big Man 54
London 42–43, 78, 112
Lone, John 106
Los Angeles 7, 47–49, 79, 81
Los Angeles Times 73–74, 93, 99
Losey, Joseph 86
Lubitsch, Ernst 112
Lucas, George 48
Lynch, Kelly 108

McCarthy, Todd 73
McGraw, Ali 67
McQueen, Steve 54, 67
Mafia 107
Magnum Force 49, 102, 103
Mansfield, David 81
Mansfield College, Oxford 11–12, 17–18, 32, *36–39*, 42, 75
Marxism 17
Masur, Richard 60
Meccano 118
MGM 76, 78, 98, 106, 108
Michelangelo 82
Michigan State University 47, 49, 80
Milchan, Arnon 108, 109
Milius, John 103
Milland, Ray 40
Milne, Tom 99–100
Montana 25n, 49, 69–71, 73–74, 84, 87, 103
Moss Bros 15

Naked Hollywood 7
National Film Theatre, London 100
New College Lane, Oxford

28–32, *31*, 42, 75
New York 76, 77, 79, 81
New York Daily News 89
New York magazine 89
The New York Times 88, 92
Newsweek 7, 92
Norman, Barry 42
Norrington, Sir Thomas 15n
nouvelle vague films 48
The Observer 95–96, 99–100
One from the Heart 78
Ordinary People 78
Orion Pictures 52, 68, 73, 89
Oscars 6, 50, 69, 78, 81, 82, 86, 105
Oxford Films 7
Oxford Times 10, 11
Oxford Union 11
Oxford University Press 112, 117

Panavision 18–19, *20*, 50, 82
Pantheon Films 53
Peckinpah, Sam 83, 95
Pergamon Press 14
Pickford, Mary 52
Pinewood Studios, Denham 12–15, 18, 75
Pink Panther films 52
Pollock, Norman 12, 13, 40
Post, Ted 103
Preminger, Otto 86
Private Life of Sherlock Holmes 15
Puzo, Mario 107

Queen's Lane, Oxford 29, 32, 43, 75

Radcliffe Infirmary, Oxford 14, 29
Radcliffe Square, Oxford 28–29
Raging Bull 78
Reagan, Ronald 95
Redford, Robert 78
Rhodes scholar 7
Ridler, Anne (VR's wife) 12, 27, 28–29, 33, *110*, 113, 115, 118

Ridler, Ben (VR's son) 112, 114, 115
Ridler, Colin (VR's son) 112, 114–16
Ridler, Vivian 6
  Diary of an Extra 8
  auditions as extra 11–12
  costume fitting 12–17
  first shoot 17–27, *23*
  second shoot 28–31, *30*, 75
  third shoot 32–40, *36–37*
  sees *Heaven's Gate* 42–43
Ridler, Vivian: complete list of films 119–22
Ridler, Vivian: principal films of
  1851 110, 117–18, 121
  Adam and Eve 117, 120
  Bad Day at Big Rock 114, 119
  The Boat Race 117, 120
  The Boys Who Ate Too Much 114, 119
  Donnington Bridge 116, 119
  A Dragon's Life 116, 119
  The End of the Line 115, 120
  The Flycatchers 116–17, 121
  The Fortune Hunters 114–15, 119
  House Extension 116, 120
  Nought for Behaviour 115, 119
  St Giles Fair 116, 119
  Slipped Disc 114, 120
  The Tenant in the Tower 116, 120
  The Thirteenth Candle 114, 120
  Tip & Run 114, 119
  A Voice from the Past 115–16, 120
Rocky Mountains 69–71
Rogers, Mimi 108
Rolling Stone 89
Rosenthal, Mark 108
Roud, Richard 93–94
Rourke, Mickey 106, 108

St Mary's, Oxford 24 and n, 116
Sarris, Andrew 88
Savage, John 50, *51*, 103
Scorsese, Martin 48, 78, 83
Scott, Jane *see* Länge, Jane
Scudamore, Nick 42–43
Seda, John 109
Sellers, Peter 52
The Shadows 114
Shane 54
Shaw, Penny 75
Sheldonian Theatre, Oxford 6, 17, 18–26, *23*, *27*, 42, 75, 94
The Sicilian 102, 107, *107*, 109
Sight & Sound 93–94, 112–13
Silent Running 102
Snagg, John 117
Some Like It Hot 52, 68
The Spectator 96–98
Spielberg, Steven 48, 50, 82
Stamp, Terence 107
Star Wars 78
Stephens, Robert 15
Stewart, James 114
Stolber, Dean 72
Stone, Oliver 106
Storaro, Vittorio 81
Stravinsky, Igor 115
Streep, Meryl 105
Streisand, Barbra 83
Stroheim, Erich von 95
Sturges, John 114
Sturges, Preston 113
Sunchaser 102, 108–109, *109*

Tarantino, Quentin 106
Tent City 32, 40
Thailand 14, 50, 105
Thomas, Kevin 93
Thomson, David 50–51
Thunderbolt and Lightfoot 49, 67, *67*, 73, 87, 102, 103

Time magazine 49, 74
Tobias, Scott 101
Tom Jones 52
Tom Tower, Oxford 42, 43
Tracey, Spencer 114
Transamerica 52–53, 68, 69, 76
Trumbull, Douglas 102
Trump, Donald 101
Twelve Angry Men 52
20th Century Fox 67, 72, 74, 107
2001: A Space Odyssey 81, 102

United Artists (UA) 81, 83, 86, 103, 106
  budget overspend on *Heaven's Gate* 6, 7, 15 and n, 25n, 50, 53, 68–74, 83, 89, 105
  buys *Heaven's Gate* script 55
  chronology of *Heaven's Gate* 67–79
  MGM buys 98
  shortened version of *Heaven's Gate* 99
  Transamerica buys 52–53
Universal Pictures 50, 52, 102, 105
Universal Studios 7

Vallely, Jean 81, 89
Variety 7
Vasconcellos, Josefina de 116
Vela, Roseanne 25
Verhoeven, Paul 86
Vernède, Andy 116
Vernède, Nicky 116
Victoria, Queen *110*, 118
Vidal, Gore 107
Vietnam War (1954–75) 50, 52, 69, 103–105
The Village Voice 88
Visconti, Luchino 96

Wajda, Andrzej 86
Walken, Christopher *Frontispiece*, *46*, 50, 58, *61*, 72, 85, 96, 97, 103, 105
Wallace, Idaho *59*, 71
Warner Brothers 72, 103, 109
Washburn, Deric 50, 102, 103
Waterston, Sam 59
Watson, Ella 55, 59–64
Wayne, John 68, 69
Welles, Orson 95
West Side Story 52, 68
Weston-super-Mare, Somerset 29 and n
Whistler, Daniel 42–43 and n
Whistler, Laurence 42n
White, Fred 14
The Wild Bunch 54
Wilder, Billy 15
Willwerth, James 74
Wilson, Dan (VR's grandson) 33 and n
Wilson, Kate (VR's daughter) 33 and n, 112, 114
Wilson, Toby (VR's grandson) 33 and n
Wyler, William 108
Wyoming 25n, 42, 54–55, 58–9, 71, 94, 95–96, 97

Yale University 47, 49, 80
Year of the Dragon 102, 106, *106*
Yesterdays 102

Zimbabwe 17
Zinner, Peter 105
Zsigmond, Vilmos 6, 19–20, 31, 34, 50, *51*, 55, 79, 81, 82–83, 94, 95